INTERPRETING ISO 9000 FOR SERVICES

SOLUTIONS FROM REGISTERED ORGANIZATIONS

C.W. Russ Russo
Tracy Callaway Russo

QUALITY RESOURCES®

A Division of The Kraus Organization Limited
New York, New York

Most Quality Resources books are available at quantity discounts when purchased in bulk. For more information contact:

Special Sales Department
Quality Resources
A Division of the Kraus Organization Limited
902 Broadway   800-247-8519
New York, New York 10010   212-979-8600
www.qualityresources.com   E-mail: info@qualityresources.com

Printed in the United States of America

02 01 00 99 98   10 9 8 7 6 5 4 3 2 1
∞
The paper used in this publication meets the minimum requirements of American National Standard for Information Sciences-Permanence of Paper for Printed Library Materials, ANSI Z39.48-1984.

ISBN 0-527-76336-5

Library of Congress Cataloging-in-Publication Data

Russo, C. W. Russ
    Interpreting ISO 9000 for services : solutions from registered organizations / C.W. Russ Russo, Tracy Callaway Russo.
        p.   cm.
    Includes index.
    ISBN 0-527-76336-5 (alk. paper)
    1. Service industries—Quality control. 2. Quality assurance—Standards. 3. Quality control—Standards. 4. ISO 9000 Series Standards. I. Russo, Tracy Callaway. II. Title.
HD9980.5.R865   1998
658.5'62—dc21   98-22825
                                                      CIP

Contents

~~⇜ ⇝~~

Preface

Congratulations. As a service practitioner interested in ISO 9000—evidenced by the fact you are reading this book—you are on the leading edge of a powerful movement to improve outcomes for service companies. It's an exciting place to be, full of opportunities to enhance competitiveness and achieve organizational objectives. In the United States, these ideas about ISO are relatively new. Compared to adoption levels of ISO 9000 around the world, the United States, so far, is an also-ran. In the United States approximately 20,000 companies are registered to ISO. Of these, only about 1,200 are service-related companies. This definitely puts you on the leading edge of this movement.

That is not to suggest service organizations have not been interested or involved in quality-related movements. In fact, service companies have and continue to adopt and use a wide variety of quality tools, and several professional organizations are devoted to quality initiatives. Team-based problem solving, process improvement, and continuous improvement methodologies are just some of the quality initiatives well represented in service companies. Many service companies have internal quality award programs, and more than 40 states have quality award programs similar to the Malcolm Baldrige National Quality Award. In all of these settings, service-related companies are well represented.

So the question must be asked: Why have so few companies adopted the ISO standards or sought ISO registration? Part of the reason is that the standard was originally written from a manufacturing perspective. The terminology barrier has hindered service organizations from understanding the benefits and inherent advantages of applying ISO 9000 principles to their work flows and processes. On the surface, the language seems to require a rigid, highly-documented system that stifles creativity. In addition, service companies—like many manufacturers—have been put off by some common misconceptions and myths surrounding the ISO movement. Finally, ISO is not a U.S.-based system and the "not invented here" mentality has deterred some companies.

In our consulting practice, and as evidenced by the case studies reported in this book, these attitudes are changing. Misconceptions and difficulties are being debunked and overcome. Service companies are discovering the advantages and benefits of seeking ISO registration. For some, ISO registration is a way to begin a quality management process in their company. For others with existing programs, ISO is a way to draw together existing initiatives and consolidate gains. And for still others, ISO will provide a foundation on which to build a world-class quality organization en route to seeking a state or national quality award such as the Malcolm Baldrige National Quality Award.

This book was written to overcome some of the barriers resulting from focus and terminology, to give practitioners in service organizations a field guide to help them understand the value of ISO and to integrate it into their organizations. The discussion and interpretations function as a guide to help service providers understand the language and apply the requirements. The case studies demonstrate practical examples of how leading-edge companies are doing this in their organizations.

The first four chapters furnish background information about ISO and registration.

- In Chapter 1, we present an overview of the International Organization for Standardization and the concepts underlying the ISO standard, how it came about, and the basic philosophical ideas fundamental to the standard.
- In Chapter 2, we describe some of the benefits of ISO 9000 registration and show the advantages it provides service organizations as well as manufacturing organizations.

- Chapter 3 describes a typical 18- to 24-month program a service company can use to develop a project plan to achieve ISO registration. We also include a discussion on how to form a team and its duties to achieve registration.
- Chapter 4 addresses some common misconceptions and false rumors about ISO. Any new idea or movement—especially when it effects change in organizations—is liable to be feared and become subject to misinformation. ISO has generated its share of misinformation and apprehension. This chapter is designed to help dispel some of the more blatant errors.

Chapters 5 through 24 each examine one of the 20 elements or sections of the ISO 9001 standard. Each chapter includes the following:

- *Key Questions.* Two or three practical questions capture the fundamental concept underlying the requirements of the section.
- *Interpreting the Standard.* This section summarizes what the section requires of any organization.
- *Service Perspectives on the Section.* This section translates the requirements of the section into service-oriented language and suggests ways to interpret the requirements in service settings.
- *Practical Examples.* Several specific and practical examples of how to interpret and apply the language in service settings are suggested in this section of the chapter.
- *Complying With the Section in Service Companies.* Here are several ideas, strategies, and tactics service organizations can use to apply the particular requirements to their work flows and processes.
- *A Service Organization Case Study.* Each case study describes how an ISO-registered service company formulated a way to conduct their business to meet the section requirements. These case studies were developed from interviews with ISO-registered service companies who generously shared their time and ideas with the authors. Individual interviewees and their companies are listed in Appendix D.
- *Lessons Learned.* The final section of each chapter strives to recapitulate the lessons the organization learned. Further, it offers a reality check, including related issues that provide the reader with some additional insight into practical concerns they might face.

The final two chapters look at life after registration and offer information and resources about the revisions to the ISO standards expected in late 2000 or early 2001. Becoming ISO-registered is a capstone event for a company. However, ISO does not end once the certificate of registration is awarded. The company must continue to maintain and improve its quality assurance process. The registrar continues to conduct surveillance—or miniaudits—every six months for the three-year life of its contract and beyond. This chapter discusses ways to maintain enthusiasm and commitment to ISO. Appendixes and an index are included to help practitioners find additional information to support their ISO implementation project that we hope the reader will find useful.

The International Organization for Standardization is planning some significant changes to the structure of its standards and guidelines, to be issued as the Year 2000 ISO 9000 family of standards. Although there will be structural changes, the basic requirements will remain essentially the same. The planned changes are designed to make the documents more user-friendly and acceptable to a broader range of organizations. The final chapter provides an overview of the work under way and presents resources to help quality practitioners remain abreast of these changes.

ACKNOWLEDGMENTS

To teach is to learn. To interview is to understand. To write is to discover.

We want to thank everyone who helped us with this book, particularly those individuals working in ISO-registered service companies who contributed their time, knowledge, and experience to the development of the individual case studies. Their generosity of spirit, unfailing enthusiasm, and cooperation have enhanced this book and added greatly to our understanding of how ISO contributes to service organizations.

Part I

This part of the book contains a brief overview to provide a framework for service practitioners as they approach planning and executing an ISO registration project. These chapters highlight some of the most salient and important ideas for service companies gleaned from our experience and the extensive general information about ISO 9000 and the registration process.

1

Overview

In 1987, the International Organization for Standardization in Geneva, Switzerland, issued the first version of the ISO 9000 series of standards and guidelines in response to a request from the European Common Market. The countries of the EC had asked the standards organization to devise a way to harmonize (the word *iso* is Greek for harmonize) the various quality assurance standards from the EC member countries so that they could eliminate redundant and, in some cases, conflicting requirements between customers and vendors in their different member countries. The ISO 9001 Quality Assurance Standard, a simple 10-page document, satisfies that request. It asks a company to address and control 20 specific issues to ensure they have in place a thorough quality assurance process.

The ISO 9000 series serves as a vehicle for communication between customers and vendors. The basic assumption underlying the ISO standards is that a good quality assurance process will satisfy customer needs by reducing nonconformance in products and services. This simple idea has proven to be so compelling that the ISO 9000 series is now used by companies in 110 countries around the world. Companies use the series to:

- Establish a system for assuring the quality of their products
- Reduce costs by improving processes
- Facilitate their supplier qualification processes
- Improve their position in the marketplace (particularly the international market)

The original writers of the standard were primarily interested in manufacturing activities, and this has caused some initial difficulties for service organizations. This is because most of the language in the series has origins in manufacturing terminology, and the issues to address appear to be production issues. Until recently, this focus on manufacturing processes has impeded service organizations from realizing the benefits and inherent advantages of applying the principles of ISO 9000 to their work flow and processes. However, many service companies now have discovered that these apparent difficulties are superficial, and they have found ways to satisfy the spirit of the requirements by interpreting the language of the standards to suit the demands of their own businesses and their own customers.

Because the standards need to be applicable to all sizes of businesses and to all types of industries, they were designed to be exceptionally generic. Essentially, the standards ask companies to address specific issues in terms of their own operations and to identify and apply strategies that meet their particular needs. However, the standards do not specify the steps a company must take to satisfy the requirements. Instead of focusing on prescribed steps, the ISO series examines the processes that ultimately create a product or service. Therefore, service organizations need only to understand the basic concept underlying each section of the standard in order to apply the requirements of the standard to their processes. This book will help companies understand the requirements of each section of the series through actual cases of how service organizations have addressed each section of the standard. In this way, the book illustrates the benefits of ISO registration and compliance.

ISO History

The use of standards to specify products and quality goes back to the guilds of the Middle Ages. The apprentice system evolved during this time to provide training to young people and thereby to establish standards of workmanship through a controlled system of guilds in such areas as silversmithing, leatherworking, and blacksmithing. Later, the first formal standards agencies were early insurance conglomerates that assessed the risks of providing insurance to shipbuilders and boilermakers. The International Organization for Standardization, in existence since 1946, has published thousands of manufacturing or product standards, similar to the Good Manufacturing Practices (GMPs) published in the United States by the American National Standards Institute (ANSI). ISO membership includes national government-sponsored standards groups and a wide variety of product-specific professional organizations. These standards agencies and product groups generate specific standards applying to individual processes or products. The U.S. member of ISO is the ANSI, the Canadian member is the Standards Council of Canada (SCC), and the United Kingdom member is the British Standards Institute (BSI).

ISO PHILOSOPHY

The two basic tenets of ISO are to satisfy customers and reduce waste. The fundamental assumption underlying this approach to quality is the belief that a structured quality assurance process will satisfy these two objectives. The ISO philosophy is that a quality product or service is produced or provided when:

- The organization's processes are well-designed to meet customer needs
- Employees understand what they must do and have the resources to perform their tasks
- Variability in the product or service is reduced, making the product or service of predictable quality

These basic ideas are developed from the classic Shewhart PDCA Cycle (Plan-Do-Check-Act), which prescribes a continuous improvement system. ISO asks companies to "Say What You Do, Do What You Say, Assess the Differences, and Improve the Processes." Companies say what they do in their quality manual, plans, procedures, and work instructions (ISO 9001 and 9002, Section 4.2). Required records (Section 4.16) provide objective evidence that demonstrates the company is doing what it says it does. The use of statistical techniques (Section 4.20), periodic management review (Section 4.1.3), and internal audits (Section 4.17) help a company assess how well their quality assurance processes are supporting their corporate strategic objectives. Control of product or service that does not meet requirements (Section 4.13) and corrective and preventive action (Section 4.14) help companies control waste and improve work processes to avoid errors. ISO focuses on preventing, rather than correcting, errors, and in providing a credible external mechanism to demonstrate to the company's constituents—customers, suppliers, distributors, competitors, and senior management—that an appropriate continuous improvement quality system is in place.

ISO STANDARDS AND GUIDELINES

ISO 9000 is actually a series of about 15 documents that include both standards and guidelines. Standards are *contract-auditable,* which means a registered company must have addressed and resolved every requirement within the standard. Registrars expect to see a quality manual that describes how the company actually applies their own processes in their own context to meet the requirements of the standard.

In contrast, guidelines are documents that provide ideas and advice to help companies interpret and apply the standards. Registrar auditors may ask questions related to the guidelines, but the guidelines contain no requirements, and auditors cannot use the guidelines to assess the company's implementation of a quality assurance process.

The three standards in the series are ISO 9001, ISO 9002, and ISO 9003. The ISO 9001 standard is the most inclusive, covering all activities from design, manufacture, and installation, to delivery and product servicing. Twenty sections or areas of concern (Sections 4.1 through 4.20) within the standard must be addressed. The specific requirements of the 9001 standard are presented as 138 *"shalls"* that a registered company is required to address. For example, the company shall have a process to qualify vendors, they shall have training records for employees, and they shall have a quality manual that describes how the company satisfies each of the requirements of the standard. ISO 9001 also requires the company to develop 18 procedures—one for each section of the standard from Section 4.3 through Section 4.20—that describe how they address each one of the concerns in each section of the standard. The company also needs to maintain a minimum of 18 kinds of records as objective evidence they have an effectively functioning quality assurance process that reduces waste or nonconformance and satisfies their customers.

The ISO 9002 matches ISO 9001 word for word except that it does not include Section 4.4, Design Control. Companies that do not have engineering or design functions may elect to register to ISO 9002. ISO 9002 contains 19 sections and 119 shalls. It requires 17 procedures and 16 records. Because many service organizations do not contain a design function, they may consider registering to ISO 9002. That option is not available to engineering consulting firms, training organizations, or to software development companies due to their strong design component. The ISO 9002 standard also is not appropriate for management consultants or any company that designs or tailors its service to individual customers. For example, a health insurance company that designs different insurance products and services for various business clients has a significant design function.

The ISO 9003 standard focuses primarily on receiving and final inspections and is usually used by distribution companies and shippers who control product in their possession but who do not perform a manufacturing activity that alters the product. The ISO 9003 standard is little used and is scheduled to be eliminated after the year 2000.

The remaining documents in the ISO 9000 series are guidelines. These are useful aids to help practitioners interpret and apply the standards. For example, ISO 9004-2 is a guideline for service organizations to use to interpret and apply the standards. The current edition of the Guideline for Services was published in 1991, and a revision is not scheduled to be released until at least 2000. The existing service organization guideline, like the other ISO guidelines, is extremely generic and presents a broad overview of service methodologies. Consistent with the ISO approach, the guideline provides limited detail on how to apply individual standard requirements to a service organization. Moreover, like many guidelines, the organization and structure of the document is confusing. The International Organization for Standardization has recognized this problem and is revising all of its guidelines to follow the structure and numbering system established for the standards. This book was prepared to provide detailed guidance for service organizations and to demonstrate through the case studies how service companies actually apply ISO to their specific needs.

There also are other useful guidelines outside the ISO 9000 series.

For example, the ISO 10011, Guidelines for Auditing Quality Systems, provides help to meet the requirements of Section 4.17 of ISO 9001, Internal Quality Audits. It describes a structure to organize and manage such a program. There also are guidelines to help companies write quality manuals and procedures, conduct corrective and preventive action programs, and apply practices to a variety of products, industries, and types of companies. New guidelines are periodically added to the series. For example, ISO Z1.11, Guideline for the Application of the ISO 9000 to Education and Training Institutions, was approved and published in August 1996.

Standards and guidelines are written and revised every five years by technical writing committees of ISO. Membership in these committees is voluntary and open to experts and interested persons from among the member nation organizations. Initial and revised draft standards and guidelines are submitted to the broader membership for comment. The approval process is sometimes long and convoluted because the technical writing committee must attempt to satisfy the varied needs of their international membership and produce documents that will be supported by all member countries. Additionally, standards are published in many languages, and the writers must structure the information so that the translations maintain the meaning and intent of the writers.

Although documents are usually revised and published every five years, there was a seven-year lag between the original 1987 version and the 1994 version of the ISO 9000 standards. This delay resulted from the explosion of worldwide interest in and a large number of comments to the writing committee in reference to the original ISO 9000 standards. Similarly, there will be a six- or seven-year lag between the 1994 edition and the planned Year 2000 ISO 9000 family of standards, currently scheduled for release in late 2000 or early 2001. The new series of standards will contain basically the same requirements, with some important structural changes to make the documents more user-friendly. The writing committee is concerned about remaining true to the basic intent and purposes already established. Some changes are likely to help clarify the requirements. There is also some discussion concerning additional requirements that are being considered. For example, the 1987 version of the ISO 9001 standard did not include a requirement for quality planning. Instead, planning had been included in one of the guidelines. The writers then included this requirement in the 1994 version of the standard. Similarly, some of the ideas currently contained in the guidelines may be added to the standard in 2000. Chapter 26 contains a discussion of the planned Year 2000 ISO 9000 family of standards, and lists some resources that will help service quality practitioners keep abreast of these changes.

Companies may either register as having satisfied the requirements of the ISO 9000 series or they may unofficially comply with the requirements. In the first situation, they become registered by going through a formal contracted audit process with an accredited ISO registrar and receive a certificate of registration. These companies then are listed by the registrar as having successfully completed the process and as having a quality management system in place that meets the requirements established in the standard. In the second scenario, companies become compliant with the standard. That is, they develop a quality management system that meets the requirements of the standard but they do not go through the formal registration process. These companies use the standard as a self-assessment tool against which to judge themselves, as baseline criteria for a good quality management program, and as a foundation for effective and efficient processes. Still other companies use the ISO standard as a means to establish a strong quality system en route to entering a corporate, state, or national award program such as the Shingo Prize, the Malcolm Baldrige National Quality Award, or various state quality awards. ISO itself is not an award, and no scores are reported for its performance. Any company that satisfies the requirements established in the standard can become registered to ISO.

The ISO 9000 series of standards and guidelines are useful for both manufacturing and service organizations. Although the series originated in manufacturing environments and much of the terminology is manufacturing-oriented, service companies are discovering the merits of adopting the ISO framework to their needs. Like manufacturers, service organizations can achieve ISO registration or compliance in order to improve their marketing efforts or to improve their internal operating effectiveness and efficiency. The primary cost advantage, however, is achieving effectiveness and efficiency.

2

The Benefits of ISO 9000

The specific advantages gained by adherence to the ISO standard can be organized into two broad categories. First, the standard helps organizations accomplish their work more effectively and efficiently. ISO does this by helping both management and employees understand what their company goals are, how they do their work, what their reasonable expectations for performance are, and how they can recognize they have successfully attained their goals. Second, registration serves as a recognizable standard for senior managers, sales representatives, and marketing personnel to use with existing and potential customers to differentiate the company from its competition. ISO registration is a powerful assurance that a company has established a recognized quality system and its processes are in control. ISO is a way for companies to enhance functional control and develop a competitive advantage.

The basic concept underlying the ISO standards for organizations is very simple: To provide accurate and effective products or services that satisfy customers' desires. This basic quality philosophy is based on the premise that companies succeed when they meet this objective and they thereby improve their chances of increasing their profitability. This idea is not a new one; it has been put forth by many well-established quality and management theorists. W. Edwards Deming argued that reducing errors reduces costs, satisfies customers, and leads to profitability. Joseph Juran promoted the idea that processes in control reduce waste and provide customers with the products and services people need. Philip Crosby promotes the idea that quality is free. That is, resources spent on management and quality initiatives have a payoff in profitability. Crosby says the real cost of quality is *unquality*, which is the cost associated with lost opportunity and waste. All of the various quality philosophies and approaches, from quality circles through self-managed matrixed teams to the ISO series, are based on the same basic goal—to harness employees' energy and enthusiasm by providing useful structures to support their productivity. The language of the ISO standard captures it: "the requirements specified are aimed primarily at achieving customer satisfaction by preventing nonconformity at all stages from design through to servicing."

ISO has been particularly useful for companies who sell their products and services to other companies. Vendors of manufactured products have discovered that ISO registration is an excellent marketing tool that gives them a competitive edge in the marketplace. Marketing staff facing increasingly stiff competition from ISO-registered companies, particularly in European and other international markets, have motivated their corporations to obtain registration in order to maintain or gain market position. Although ISO registration is not a legislatively or legally mandated requirement anywhere in the world, throughout Europe—and increasingly today in the United States—lack of registration is becoming a competitive disadvantage.

Large corporations, such as the Big Three automakers and such high-technology companies as AT&T, as well as companies in some other industries, have been in the forefront of seeking ISO registration for themselves and demanding registration from all the companies that provide products and services to them. Automobile makers competing in the United States against foreign car makers have adopted a more stringent version of the ISO standards. Their QS-9000 includes the text of the ISO standard plus additional requirements particular to the automotive industry. There are several reasons why these large companies demand that vendors be registered. First, doing business with registered companies helps to satisfy the requirements of ISO Section 4.6, Purchasing, which requires that ISO-registered companies have an established method to qualify vendors. Qualifying vendor capability can be done by assessing the vendor's quality assurance system. One of the easiest ways for an ISO-registered company to do this assessment is to limit purchases only to ISO-registered vendors. This is based on the belief that a vendor's in-control quality assurance program typically helps eliminate problems. This belief helps buyers gain confidence that the vendor will provide a good product or service.

Industrial customers have traditionally tried various ways to ensure that their vendors provide suitable products and services. They have developed a variety of methods to qualify vendors, particularly in situations when an unsatisfactory vendor's product has the potential to cause a defect or failure in their own company's product. Large buyers have traditionally dispatched their own quality personnel to audit and judge vendors' and potential vendors' capability before placing an order. Similarly, many departments and agencies throughout the U.S. government maintain large staffs of regulatory inspectors or quality control auditors involved in their procurement chain. One of the major advantages accruing to large company purchasing programs that demand vendors be ISO-registered companies is that, in many cases, they are able to reduce their cost of vendor qualification oversight or inspection. By requiring vendors to obtain and maintain ISO 9000 registration, these large customers have been able to shift the cost of verification activities from their procurement budgets and to lay off those costs onto their vendors.

Although vendors have had to bear their own costs of obtaining ISO registration, in many cases that is an advantage because they no longer must host "visiting firemen" from many of their customer companies who want to conduct audits of their facilities. The vendors simply register and adhere to the ISO requirement, rather than deal individually with multiple customer requirements. In some cases, vendors must have separate quality systems to deal with conflicting customer requirements. Their ISO registration has allowed these vendors to focus all of their energy into their ISO program, which, over the long term, is a less expensive alternative than dealing with customers individually.

ISO registration is not entirely a question of marketability and competitive pressures, as is demonstrated by the many companies that have decided to become compliant to the standard without going through the final step of becoming formally registered. These companies recognize the need to improve work flows and processes in order to drive down costs. They have decided to become compliant to the requirements of the standard because they perceive the 20 sections of the standard to be a model to effectively and efficiently organize how they go about routine daily tasks.

THE BENEFITS OF ISO TO SERVICE ORGANIZATIONS

Service organizations have been relatively slow to adopt the ISO principles to their own operations. A number of reasons contribute to this:

- The language in ISO is primarily manufacturing-oriented, and the applicability of the terminology appears somewhat foreign to service organizations.
- The structure of the standard focuses on processes and structures that have not been well understood in service organizations. Many service organizations fear that structured processes may hinder flexibility and creativity and reduce reaction time in changing markets.
- Service organizations that typically offer their service to the general public—rather than to other corporations—have not been motivated to seek registration because members of the general public do not understand how ISO registration directly affects them.

However, despite these issues and concerns, service providers are more similar to than different from product manufacturers.

Service and manufacturing companies have in common the need to define a strategic direction and purpose for their business; employ people and resources to produce the product or provide the service; establish work flows to control processes; apply measures that assess results and guide their business; and need a mechanism to assure that customers receive exactly what they expect. Regardless of type of service provided, management style, organizational culture, company size, or operating environment, service organizations can follow ISO's requirements to realize the same process improvement, cost reduction, and marketing advantages manufacturers have discovered. This is because ISO focuses on the processes involved in providing the services, and not directly at the end result. Every business activity can be thought of as a process, and the factors that help a process work effectively can be identified, controlled, and improved. Consider, for example, the process of conducting successful meetings. Such meetings are based on several factors, including a controlled agenda, a clearly specified goal or objective, attenders who understand and practice good meeting skills, and facilitators who are able to draw contributions from all attenders while keeping the meeting on track. A productive meeting thus is in many ways like a well-run factory assembly line. Participants in both settings know what they are trying to achieve and have the skills and knowledge to get the job done. Although the assembly line is highly structured and the interactions in a meeting allow creative contributions, both succeed based on a set of expectations and rules that can be learned and followed.

Large, well-established service processes, such as backroom operations in a bank or claims processing in a health insurance company, may seem most suitable for ISO because their operations are controlled and process-oriented, rather like the manufacturing operations for which ISO originally was established. For example, Health Risk Management, Inc., has two major operations and several smaller regional offices for processing health claims. As seen in the case study in Chapter 13, they used the standard to structure how they conduct their backroom claim processing operations. However, small, entrepreneurial service organizations operating in rapidly changing environments will gain similar benefit from applying ISO standard requirements to their operations. Both Applied Consumer and Clinical Evaluations (Chapter 12) and International Language Engineering (Chapter 14) operate in highly charged and rapidly changing environments. They have used the standard to help them maintain their balance and focus in these kinds of highly charged and changing environments. Also, large organizations with branch offices, or technology-based organizations that rely on external support with such components as teleworkers, independent contractors, or outsourced suppliers, find ISO beneficial. For these organizations, ISO provides mechanisms to effectively organize, coordinate, and control dispersed activities, which is perhaps their greatest challenge. In the same way, service organizations based primarily on point-of-contact customer interactions that require spontaneous responses to meet a given situation can benefit from ISO's approach to understanding and organizing processes to meet organizational needs. For example, as seen in the case studies of the medical practice of Drs. Figgie and Larkin (Chapter 10) and the real estate firm of Mary Kay Hopkins (Chapter 22), small companies that provide one-on-one service can benefit from structuring how they provide their services to their customers.

The ISO standard asks companies to describe, for each of its 20 sections, the processes they use to achieve success. The act of describing the process forces management to carefully describe and communicate expected performance levels and parameters within which personnel can and should operate. Processes are described as procedures. Some service providers incorrectly have perceived the need for procedures as a requirement to anticipate all possible iterations and potential situations and to describe every appropriate response. Complex procedures covering every eventuality are impossible either to create or implement. They stifle creativity and hinder processes by freezing freedom to act and demoralizing personnel. ISO registration does not require complex procedures. In fact, some companies have challenged themselves to develop very short procedures using a flowchart to describe the primary steps in a process. These kinds of procedures give employees great freedom to exercise creativity and responsibility to accomplish goals and to resolve problems within established authority. For example, ISO procedures can help service repair technicians understand their tasks and what they can do to help customers—particularly what concessions they can make for customers—to restore service quickly. Clearly defined responsibilities and authorities help sales personnel and customer service personnel respond to customer needs. A good contract review process—as required by Section 4.3 of the standard—helps salespersons feel confident that the promises they make to customers are possible to deliver. Such confidence equals good service and ensures that the right product or service is delivered on time and as promised—in the language of the standard, "as specified." Good processes also help workers do a good job. For example, established expectations and work processes help telecommuters establish lines of communication with their organizations and provide clear guidance of what is expected and how to succeed in this work setting.

The real advantage of ISO registration or compliance is that it gives management and employees a framework within which to operate. Done well, such frameworks encourage flexibility while providing needed structures to support employees as they work to deliver a good service. ISO provides a framework within which customer service personnel can effectively and efficiently diagnose issues and direct customers to needed solutions. For example a health insurance company may establish a "Dial a Nurse" program to help individuals diagnose health issues and direct them to an appropriate health care provider. Such a program cannot succeed without a solid structure and such problem-solving tools as a diagnosis decision tree. Becoming registered to ISO helps service companies recognize the utility these kinds of tools provide their employees to help them do a good job. A reasonable outcome—and return on investment for the dollars spent on registration—for an ISO service company is improved operational effectiveness and efficiency. The resources invested in ISO are the same resources companies should be devoting to process improvements regardless of their decision to seek ISO registration.

Regardless of the company's style and culture—whether severely structured or creative and freewheeling work—the range of organizational contexts in which ISO works can be seen in a comparison of a company using self-directed teams and one comprised of individual service representatives dealing with customer needs. In a self-directed, matrixed process improvement team, the basic rules may include specifically identifying metrics and stakeholders, achieving goals within the group itself, and using a disciplined problem-solving step approach based on quality tools. Such a structure and approach fits well within an ISO-registered framework. At the same time, ISO can describe the processes employees use while interacting with customers in a one-on-one situation. They are dealing with the same general concepts. Just like the matrix team, they need the skills and knowledge to be able to effectively provide the service. These customer service employees also need to understand the parameters of their authority and responsibility to achieve excellent customer service. Well-planned processes help employees recognize what they must and can do to provide good service.

OVERCOMING THE DIFFERENCES

Some problems may arise from differences between products and services, although many of these differences are superficial and can be surpassed by recognizing some basic similarities. For example, although products are tangible and a service provided is intangible, both have associated costs and require that there be a defined and structured way for employees to be able to produce the product or provide the service. ISO helps service organizations structure how they provide their service. This structure supports quality service by helping the employees who provide the service to understand customer needs, their roles, and the company's expectations of them. The wide variety of organizational structures and methods used in both service industries and product industries reflect the particular nature of the product or service provided. For example, there are vast differences between the requirements and processes involved in manufacturing high-technology products verses manufacturing widgets. Similar differences exist among service providers. For example, the individual who maintains complex automated blood analysis equipment has a vastly different task than the individual who draws the blood from a patient. Regardless of these differences, however, both employees need to understand their work and work within a system that allows them to succeed in their tasks. The development of structure that ISO compliance brings to their activities is one of its major advantages.

One of the most critical differences between products and services is that, in face-to-face service contexts, there is no opportunity to correct a nonconformance or to fix a problem once the failure in service has occurred. In contrast, a manufacturer has several opportunities to control the quality of the product before it goes to the customer, by carefully controlling the production process, measuring the results, and inspecting for errors before shipment. A service provider does not have the luxury of this production interval, since the service is rendered in real time. If there is an error as the service is being provided, the damage is done, and the service provider then must make reparations and corrections in front of the customer. Service providers who avoid problems and service failures and who are able to reduce variations or waste and errors as they provide their service gain a significant financial savings as well as earning customer satisfaction and loyalty. An ISO structure will help service companies accomplish this goal.

Another critical difference is that product producers typically try to drive out variation in their products. Their customers expect each item in a batch or each item in their product line to meet identical requirements. In contrast, service providers routinely deal with a high degree of variability, and the service must meet the particular needs of individual customers. Many service providers incorrectly perceive that ISO will require them to standardize how they do business and reduce their capability to deal creatively and in an appropriate time frame with variability. ISO requires service providers to formulate structures within which employees will work and to provide employees with the tools and resources to effectively handle and satisfy customers. However, ISO does not require standardization of services, only that the service provider think through its strategy and tactics to obtain its desired strategic results. Then the service provider must put into place a framework within which employees can work to achieve those goals. ISO does not require conformity. It does not, however, tolerate improvisation. ISO done correctly definitely will not inhibit creativity and flexibility.

Some managers who are most comfortable with linear relationships between investment and results find it challenging to attribute financial outcomes to resources spent on service. This creates pressure to minimize expenditures on service. In some situations, as a result, the point of contact between the customer and the company—the most important transaction point—is filled by the youngest, least well-paid, and least-trained individuals. In contrast, such companies frequently will spend significant resources on machinery and equipment in order to ensure the product is manufactured according to specifications. Some managers similarly have the mistaken belief that somehow service is not as difficult to organize and provide as a manufactured product. However, an ISO-compliant service is able to demonstrate the complexity of its tasks and generate fact-based justifications for the resources it spends to achieve excellent service. With this as a basis, it is possible for a company to determine and to demonstrate the financial gains they accrue as a result of their ISO quality management system.

The similarity between manufacturers and service providers is highlighted by the services many manufacturers offer their customers. For example, a computer manufacturer may provide technical support services for its customers. In fact, manufacturers have had little difficulty incorporating into their ISO registration the services they offer along with their products. Within the universe of registered companies, there are multiple examples of successful service providers within manufacturing companies. A scan through the list of registered companies shows that many of their scopes of registration also include service to their customers. For example, the Lake Charles Plant PPG Industries, Inc. (Chapter 17) is a service provider within a production organization. In addition, every company has internal customers, those departments or functions that must interact and help each other to support the business. The training function within BC TELECOM, Inc. (Chapter 11) is such a provider of internal service to their organization. In one way or another, every organization contains critical service functions.

MARKETING SERVICES WITH ISO

The second broad category of advantages of ISO for service organizations focuses on the marketing advantage ISO registration provides. Such marketing advantages include marketing to both internal and external customers. Registration represents certification by a recognized third party that an organization has met the requirements of the standard and, therefore, it has a solid quality program in place. This provides advantages in advertising, marketing and sales, and in helping an individual group within the organization demonstrate their corporate contribution. Many of the case study participants reported that they believed they had a good quality program in place before starting on their ISO registration project. Their ISO programs provided a foundation upon which to build and improve existing programs. For example, the United Package Service Package Lab (Chapter 19) is part of a company that has had a quality vision since 1907. Their motto then was, "The Best Service at the Lowest Rates."

Essentially, third-party or extrinsic ISO registration allows a service company to have an outside, unbiased evaluation of the quality management system in place within an organization. The concept underlying ISO registration is very similar to the concept of conducting a financial audit by one of the major accounting firms. In both situations, there are acceptable practices and standards to be met. The accounting auditor—or ISO registrar—provides an unbiased assessment and verification that the company meets the established standards.

ISO registration will help a service company market itself in at least three ways. First, registration can be a powerful marketing and advertising point. Second, registration helps service vendors qualify to bid for business. And, third, registration provides groups or functions within companies a way to demonstrate the value of their services within their own companies.

Marketers use their ISO registration in sales presentations, advertising materials, on letterheads and corporate information brochures, and in product information. If the competition is not registered, sales force personnel can use their registration as a significant way to distinguish their organization from the competition. If the competition is registered, the salespersons can use their own company's registration as an indication that the competition has no advantage in the area.

The second marketing advantage focuses on how vendors and subcontractors can be qualified to bid or provide services to their customer companies. This advantage comes directly from the ISO standard itself. Section 4.6, Purchasing, requires ISO-registered companies to qualify vendors on the basis of that vendor's ability to meet contract requirements. The standard says that one way to qualify a vendor is to judge the vendor's quality assurance system. Obviously, one way for an ISO-registered company to meet this requirement is to insist that all of its own vendors be ISO-registered.

A final advantage for ISO registration or compliance may accrue to an individual organizational component, such as an individual workgroup or function, and particularly for a service function within a larger organization. Registration or compliance gives the managers of such a component group a way to demonstrate the value of the services they provide to the company. Too frequently, senior organizational executives focus on the cost of capital or machinery, return on investment, sales per full-time-equivalent employee, or other easily obtained metrics. They also need to have access to measurements and other evidence that support the expenditure of resources in the "soft" internal services such as training, sales, accounting, and quality, among others. ISO compliance in these internal service functions helps senior managers apply the same familiar measurement- and outcome-focused approach to these soft services. Compliance gives internal services elements a way to structure and measure and, therefore, to demonstrate their contribution to the company's overall strategic goals.

ISO registration or compliance is a major, resource-intensive undertaking. To justify the expenditure of resources, service practitioners must understand the costs of quality and the return on investment in seeking ISO registration. From both marketing and process improvement perspectives, the ISO standard gives service practitioners a demonstrated, measurable way to assess their own performance, improve that performance, contribute to their company's strategic goals, and, in the process, to be acknowledged for their efforts.

3

~ૐ ૐ~

How to Organize and Execute an ISO Registration Project

Instituting an ISO 9000 registration or compliance project represents a major undertaking for any organization. It is essentially a change project, with all the associated challenges and repercussions. As in any large project, many people and tasks are involved over a long time frame requiring thoughtful and thorough planning and administration. This chapter is designed to help service companies formulate a team-based approach to develop a project plan to achieve ISO registration. It is divided into two parts.

The first part describes a typical four-phase, 18- to 24-month project. There is considerable overlap among the four phases; however, this model will help practitioners plan their work. In addition, although time lines for each of the four stages vary among organizations and overlap, a six-month schedule for each phase is a reasonable estimate for initial planning. It is not possible, however, to completely overlap the four phases and complete the project in six months. An ISO registration program implies organizational change, and the process requires some gestation time for people to learn and become comfortable with the program.

The second part of the chapter identifies ISO project team participants and suggests some of their duties and responsibilities to support the registration project.

FOUR STEPS TO REGISTRATION

Phase One: Decision

The initial move toward registration involves learning about the ISO standards and guidelines and the registration process. Public seminars and books about ISO are helpful ways to gather such information. The World Wide Web is a rich resource for information. (When conducting a search, be careful to include the 9000 after the word ISO to avoid falling into sites devoted to "In Search Of.") Many community college industry outreach programs focus on helping small companies achieve registration. A number of professional organizations also sponsor ISO support groups for their members. Discussions with companies that are registered or are seeking registration will provide additional practical insight into the process. Interestingly, there is no ISO requirement for companies to benchmark their experiences with ISO. However, many registered companies are receptive to sharing their experiences, as is evident in the case studies in this book.

A primary goal during this decision stage is to determine what advantages and disadvantages the service organization expects to obtain by adopting ISO. These can be thought of as first-level objectives, those outcomes that can be clearly identified and/or measured. These may be reaching new market segments, reducing make-good expenditures, or heightening reported customer satisfaction. Keeping an organizational eye on these targets tends to help sustain senior management interest and therefore sustain allocation of necessary resources for the project. In this stage, the resource requirements and costs of the project should be identified. Launching such a project without a firm understanding of the implications, advantages and costs will, at a minimum, lead to disappointments and wasted effort.

Also, during this initial phase it is a good idea to begin developing a project plan, including establishing a proposed budget, forming an ISO implementation team, and conducting a gap or delta assessment. A gap/delta assessment will help identify the difference between what currently exists in the organization and what must be done to meet the requirements of the standard. Essentially, a gap assessment looks at the requirements of the standard and identifies what activities and structures currently exist—or that can be modified—to satisfy the ISO requirements. Many organizations discover they can use a significant amount of their currently existing processes, procedures, teams, quality programs, problem-solving and continuous improvement efforts as a foundation for their ISO program.

Phase Two: Development

Once the major tasks are identified and a proposed budget and schedule are drafted, it should then be possible to gain management approval to move into the second of the four phases. About halfway through this second phase, it is useful to finalize the budget and project plan and to gain firm management commitment to achieve registration. This is the time to schedule a tentative preassessment and the registration audit, and to begin working toward those two capstone events. These firm dates will help make the project real in everyone's mind and add momentum to the succeeding steps.

Phase Two is where most of the intense preparation work for registration is accomplished and most of the resources are spent. In Phase Two of the project, the organization's processes and procedures are identified and documentation to formalize them is begun. In this same phase, the members of the four primary teams that will drive the project should be chosen and trained. These key driver teams and their tasks are (1) internal audit, (2) corrective and preventive action, (3) documentation, and (4) records-keeping. There is a detailed discussion of the four sections of the standard covering these four topics in the chapters on Sections 4.5, Document and Data Control; 4.14, Corrective and Preventive Action; 4.16, Control of Quality Records; and 4.17, Internal Quality Audits. Volunteers can be sought or appropriate candidates appointed to the four teams. The duties and responsibilities of each team are discussed later in this chapter. The primary outcomes of this phase are the development of processes and procedures to formalize work flows, and structures to meet the requirements of the 20 sections of the ISO standard.

Toward the end of this phase, the organization should begin the process of researching and contracting with an ISO registrar. And, once most of the procedures are written, the team should begin to write the service organization's quality manual. A detailed discussion of the reasons for writing the quality manual late in this phase of the project appears in Chapter 6, Quality System.

Phase Three: Evolution

Phase Three of the project is essentially a period of evolution, in contrast to establishment and implementation in Phases One and Two. It is a time to allow employees to become comfortable with and adopt newly established work flows as part of their routine. As ISO percolates and permeates throughout the organization, opportunities for improvement will present themselves. It will also allow time to accumulate six months or so of records and objective evidence that the ISO quality management system is in place and helping the organization accomplish its corporate strategic objectives. Most registrars require a minimum of three to six months experience as evidence that the quality system is operational and effective before they will conduct a registration audit and issue a certificate of registration. Therefore, this six-month maturation period is essential for a successful registration audit. The final activities at the end of this phase are to complete the quality manual, to contract with an ISO registrar, and to conduct a preassessment registration audit.

Seventy or so registrar companies in the United States are accredited to conduct registration audits. Most have extensive experience with manufacturing and regulated industries, and many are gaining experience with service organizations. Usually, it is a three- or four-month process to find and contract with a suitable registrar. Each registrar has its own corporate personality and industry area of expertise. Service companies should do extensive research and have an established plan to select and contract with a registrar. This structured approach to selecting a registrar is in keeping with the requirements of Section 4.6, Purchasing, which requires companies to select vendors on the basis of their ability to satisfy their company's needs.

The registrar is a vendor of a service, and the company will usually sign a three-year contract with their selected registrar. Therefore, the registrar should be selected carefully. The registrar selection team should conduct its initial research from the universe of registrars by looking for registrars with service company experience. The selection team might also ask their largest and best customers for recommendations. Once the initial list is reduced down to half a dozen candidates, the team should conduct telephone and site visits to interview potential registrars. Questions about the registrar's specific experience, accreditation, billing practices, industry experience, and style and approach to ISO and the auditing process will help the team winnow the list down to one or two final candidates. In the final analysis, it will come down to how the team perceives the registrar is able to serve their company's needs.

Phase Four: Continuation

The final phase is to conduct the registration audit and to continue to maintain the ISO quality assurance system. Depending on the size of the organization, the registrar will send several auditors and spend several days at the company to do a complete audit of procedures and practices. After the audit, the company may take several weeks or months to satisfy the audit findings before receiving their certificate of registration. Once the certificate is in hand, the registered company will be listed in the national registry of ISO companies and may use the registrar's ISO logo on its stationery and in its marketing materials. After registration, the registrar will conduct semiannual audits, and the company will continue its internal audit and other ISO required processes. In essence, a company never completes ISO; they achieve registration and then must continue to adhere to, maintain, and evolve their quality assurance program. Chapter 25 discusses some ideas to maintain enthusiasm and continue to improve processes using ISO.

THE ISO IMPLEMENTATION TEAM

Because of the complex scope of an ISO 9000 implementation project, it is a good idea to involve as many people as early in the project as possible. Eventually, every employee in the organization will own a piece of ISO as it relates to their individual daily job. Involving many people will encourage them to take ownership and avoid the perception that ISO is imposed upon them. Additionally, implementation is more work than one or a few people can successfully handle while trying to maintain and attend to their other duties. It is definitely not a good idea to hire additional personnel for the sole purpose of achieving ISO registration. Registration must be achieved by the people who accomplish the daily tasks within the company. Companies that have assigned full-time individuals and thus separated the implementation process from all of the other employees have discovered that ISO becomes an unused waste of resources because the program is not integrated into the routine, daily assignments. If the implementation process has wide support, the program is owned and implemented by the individuals who created it.

A good approach is to form several teams and assign specific tasks to selected individuals to work within those teams. What follows is a description of one way to form an ISO implementation team along with team member tasks and assignments. Each organization should determine a system that meets its particular needs.

Management Representative

The ISO 9000 standard requires senior management to appoint someone from within their own management group to serve as the focal point for all ISO activities. This individual should be someone fairly high within the organization who possesses both credibility and corporate power to gain the attention and respect from all levels of management to get things done. The standard defines several duties for the Management Representative, including establishing, maintaining, and implementing the ISO process. Additionally, the Management Representative is responsible periodically to assess and report to senior management on the effectiveness of the ISO quality assurance systems. The Management Representative should be the chairperson of the ISO implementation team and work with each of the team members to help them accomplish their tasks and objectives. The Management Representative should be a high-energy, well-organized, politically astute individual able to work cooperatively with all employees within the service organization.

Internal Audit Team Members

ISO requires companies to conduct periodic assessments of their ISO process. Chapter 21, Internal Quality Audits (Section 4.17), presents a detailed discussion of these requirements for an internal audit program. A group of employees must be trained to serve as internal auditors. It is a good idea to have either 10 percent of the company or about 15 persons available to serve as internal auditors. It is also a good idea to select individuals from many different areas or departments and from a variety of hierarchy levels from within the organization. This approach will help disperse responsibility throughout the organization and avoid the perception that ISO is centered within one group or is the responsibility of one person. Additionally, because every department and function within the organization will be involved in preparing themselves for registration, the internal auditors within the respective departments can serve as resource persons to help their own functions prepare for registration.

Internal auditors conduct individual audits of all company work processes and functions to satisfy the requirements for Internal Quality Audits (Section 4.17). One way to satisfy this requirement is by assigning two or three individuals to conduct a short audit of one area or function. Short audits should be scheduled once or twice per month so that at the end of a year every function or activity has been audited at least one time against its relevant section(s) of the standard and the company's quality procedures.

Internal Audit Team Leader

The internal audit team leader is both administrator of and advisor to the internal audit team members. This individual is responsible for developing and issuing the annual audit schedule and for coordinating with the affected supervisors and department heads to ensure that audits are conducted as scheduled. The team leader also attends to all of the administrative functions, including compiling and distributing audit reports and liaison with the corrective and preventive action team leader.

The internal audit team leader frequently becomes the lightning rod for misunderstandings and discontent that may be generated by the audit process. It is important to remember that audits often are perceived by organizational members as having inherent risk to them. Therefore, the individual selected for this position should be someone with significant experience and knowledge about the company and who is able to maintain personal balance and aplomb even while presenting a nonconformance to a recalcitrant supervisor or manager.

Documentation Team

One of the basic tenets of ISO is "Say What You Do and Do What You Say." Companies say what they do in their quality manual, plans, procedures, and work instructions. Generating simple and useful procedures and work instructions to both describe and control work flows is probably one of the most difficult aspects of any implementation project. Sending a line supervisor an internal memo with instructions to produce a procedure describing the work area or activity is certainly the least effective way to generate good, usable procedures.

An alternative and much more efficient approach is to assemble a two- or three-person documentation team to work with employees to flowchart processes and develop work instructions and procedures. This approach involves employees who do the work, so they take ownership of the documents and their accuracy. Other advantages of this approach are that it ensures consistency of format and level of detail across documents, and it eliminates the need to have many employees spend time becoming knowledgeable about writing documentation. Most important, a good documentation team can produce superior documents in less than half the time and without much of the frustration that occurs when individual supervisors and managers are asked to produce them.

Corrective and Preventive Action Team

This team supports the company by managing the continuous improvement program and satisfying the standard's requirements. The support may consist of assigning several individuals from within the organization who are able to implement a disciplined problem-solving approach to identify opportunities for improvements and to resolve nonconformances and implement change. This team will work with individual supervisors and managers to resolve audit findings. However, they can also work with a variety of other inputs, including employee suggestions, customer surveys and customer complaints, trend reports, and other data to identify existing and potential problems and their root causes, and to conduct continuous improvement activities. It is a mistake to limit corrective and preventive action to only nonconformances generated by the ISO audit process. Companies do well when they assimilate data and information from a wide variety of sources and seek opportunities for improvements in a coherent and structured way.

Records Team

Many companies have excellent and sophisticated records management programs. Such well-run programs easily satisfy the ISO requirements. The requirements for record keeping specified in Control of Quality Records (Section 4.16) are fairly routine. However, they do require attention to detail and close control. These team members are charged with, first, making sure that there is a functioning records management process in place and, second, that rogue records are kept in check. Rogue records are usually generated by individuals who see the need for a security blanket by maintaining their personal copy of selected records for their personal files. Although ISO does not disallow this practice, such records must be kept in accordance with the company's established records-keeping procedure. By ISO definition, every file and every record in the company is a quality record. Frequently, the records-keeping team discovers that their initial primary task is a massive housecleaning project.

Employee Communication Team

One or two individuals should serve the project by finding frequent, short, and reliable ways to help all company employees become knowledgeable about ISO and the advantages of seeking registration. They also should provide up-to-date information and reports on the status of the implementation project. Reports in the company newsletter, postings on bulletin boards, quick blurbs in e-mail updates, payroll stuffers, and short updates in safety training or department meetings are all ways to get the word out, reduce fear and apprehension, and engage employees to support the ISO project. The team also should plan and conduct minicelebrations along the way when significant milestones are reached.

Wizards

Within every organization there are individuals who enjoy being involved in interesting undertakings that they perceive will help the company, who are unafraid and welcome change, who are early adopters of new ideas, and who are in a position to knock down barriers and to help push favored projects along to successful conclusion. The wizards may work overtly as members of the ISO oversight committee and represent the project to senior management, or they may work covertly in an informal advisory or mentoring capacity. Regardless of their status, obtaining support from these wizards is crucial to the success of an ISO implementation team.

Although some individuals thrive on change, many individuals in organizations seek familiarity, stability, and the status quo. ISO is a change project and can engender fear and apprehension in some people until they become familiar with its purpose and practice and come to perceive and appreciate the personal advantages ISO brings to them and their jobs. Even ISO enthusiasts struggle with the long-term commitment and ongoing effort to achieve and maintain registration. Additionally, most individuals engaged in an ISO implementation project are not freed from the responsibility of attending to their regular daily tasks, even while pushing through a change project.

Like most projects, the road to ISO can be full of potholes, and it is not uncommon for travelers to find themselves distracted and wandering off on tangent paths following false initiatives and starts. It would be lovely if ISO were easy and instantaneous. It's not. A team approach and solid project management practices will help the service organization reach its goal of ISO registration.

4

Myths and Misconceptions About ISO 9000

In any equivocal or rapidly changing situation, rumors and misinformation frequently surface and spread. Organizations undertaking significant change projects usually experience increased rumor activity. Sometimes, when there is insufficient information about the change and its expected effects on the operation, some individuals will simply fabricate something, generate possible scenarios, and check their likelihood with others (thereby passing this information through the organization) rather than suffer the vacuum.

On a broader scale, some pervasive myths and misconceptions continue to circulate about the ISO 9000 standards and their application. It is important to remember the standards themselves are very new, being first published in 1987. Despite their broad acceptance around the world, early misinformation about the purpose and application of the standard, which arose because of fear of change and misunderstanding of ISO requirements, continues to be repeated.

As ISO's acceptance increases among service industries, many of these same concerns and issues are surfacing again. Reviewing reports from companies interviewed for the case studies in this book and based on our own consulting experiences among service practitioners, it is clear these common myths are being perpetuated. This chapter deals with several of the more common misconceptions about ISO 9000. Companies that embark on an ISO registration or ISO transformation project are sure to hear at least some of these and possibly other rumors and errors.

MYTH 1: ISO DOESN'T IMPROVE QUALITY

Some people appear to believe that the only thing necessary to achieve and maintain ISO registration is to document and follow procedures. These skeptics argue that ISO-registered companies can offer a substandard service or produce poor-quality products as long as the company follows its own procedures.

The reality is that ISO is a quality management system based on two fundamental objectives—to satisfy the customer and to drive waste or error out of the process. Section 1.0, the Scope section of the standard, articulates the basic quality concept—the standard is "aimed primarily at achieving customer satisfaction by preventing nonconformity. . . ." ISO's focus on customer satisfaction and waste reduction is entirely consistent with most quality movements and theorists. For example, W. Edwards Deming proposed reducing waste in the system by reducing variability in processes. Reducing waste in the system drives down production costs. As costs are reduced, it is possible to both increase value for the customer and increase profits for the company. Even more fundamentally, understanding customer needs and creating a system that supports meeting those needs through efficient and effective processes assures the delivery of a quality product to the customer.

Underlying these basic concepts of meeting customer needs and reducing waste is a requirement to assess and improve processes. The internal audit (Section 4.17) and corrective and preventive action (Section 4.14) requirements reflect the same concepts expressed elsewhere in the quality literature as self-assessment and continuous improvement. These are fundamental components of the ISO philosophy and standard. The notion that ISO does not improve quality is patently incorrect.

MYTH 2: ISO IS A PAPERWORK NIGHTMARE

Unfortunately, in some companies, the fear that ISO creates a mountain of onerous paperwork and procedures has become a reality. This outcome, however, does not arise from the requirements of the standard, but rather from its interpretation and application by individual organizations. The standard clearly states that "the range and detail of the procedures that form part of the quality system shall be dependent upon the complexity of the work, the methods used, and the skills and training needed by personnel involved in carrying out the activity" (Section 4.2.2). If the work is simple, if the way the work is done is straightforward and consistent, or if knowledgeable and experienced individuals are available to do the work, there is no need for new or revised procedures or work instructions. Unfortunately, some ISO practitioners try to document every activity in such a way that every imaginable contingency is covered. This is obviously impossible. Becoming bogged down with a narrow focus on paperwork and procedural details keeps the organization from profitably spending time looking at how work flows and tasks are accomplished.

The most appropriate response to ISO requirements for documentation is to develop short, useful procedures and work instructions that:

- Ensure that best practices are followed
- Help individual employees understand what needs to be done
- Give guidance on how to accomplish tasks

The litmus test for any document is: "Do employees use it?" If the answer is yes, then the document is needed. If the answer is no, the procedure or work instruction is probably a waste of paper.

The standard does require companies to develop a procedure to explain how they address each one of the sections of the standard. At a minimum, that requirement can be satisfied with 18 procedures. There is no requirement in the standard that says how long or how detailed those procedures need to be. The company must figure out a useful way to describe their processes to satisfy the standard. Also, the company is at liberty to determine which additional procedures and work instructions they need to control their work processes. Any organization that writes too many procedures or in too much detail has called the documentation monster upon itself.

MYTH 3: ISO STIFLES CREATIVITY AND FAST RESPONSE

This myth is an outgrowth of the misconceptions, first, that employees must adhere rigidly to ISO procedures and, second, that once procedures are written and approved, they never can be changed. The standard (Section 4.1.2.1) says that procedures should empower employees who "manage, perform, and verify work"—essentially everyone in the organization—to make sure each task is done correctly, problems are identified, nonconformances are corrected, and solutions are found to improve processes. Again, the real challenge is to prepare intelligent and useful procedures and work instructions based on efficient and effective work flows and work processes. In addition, it is imperative to have a documentation change process that is inviting and easy to use to encourage employees not only to find ways to improve processes and find new ways to solve problems, but also to encourage them to update the documentation appropriately.

Myth 4: ISO Is the Quality Department's Job

ISO is a quality management system. The emphasis should be on the word *management*, even more than the word *quality*. In fact, it is possible to retain the spirit of the standard by paraphrasing the wording in the standard, deleting the word "quality", and substituting the word "management" in its place. Moreover, ISO does not belong to management. It belongs to everyone in the organization, especially to employees who actually do the work of performing the service. To be sure, ISO asks organizations to look at work flows and work processes performed by every employee, but the employees own the tasks that make up their individual jobs. They are responsible for doing their work well. ISO should help them achieve excellence in their job performance.

A related misunderstanding suggests that ISO is separate from the real work of providing the service. Some employees think they can "do ISO" separately from their jobs or that ISO is a fad with no connection to the reality of their daily concerns. ISO is not another in the long list of management or organizational improvement systems that were here today and gone tomorrow. It is not a management-guru flavor-of-the-month program. Its long-term value has been and continues to be demonstrated by its adoption by thousands of companies around the world and its support by governments, educators, professional organizations, industries, and customers.

MYTH 5: ISO IS A MAGIC PILL

The first four misconceptions were negative about ISO. The fifth myth errs on the positive side. It raises unreasonable expectations and sets up companies for disappointment. It conceives of ISO as a magic pill or panacea to solve all of an organization's problems. An organization does not live in stasis; it is impossible to cure or vaccinate it against new problems, except with the most powerful quality system. Even in a company that has achieved excellent quality service, new problems must be solved and work processes can always be improved. Mistakes will continue to be made, and service workers will continue to be frustrated when they do not live up to their own expectations and when they believe more can be achieved.

ISO acknowledges the need for and encourages ongoing incremental improvements. The only thing that does not change in its philosophy is the requirement to keep changing. ISO provides a framework and a methodology within which all the members of the organization can participate in solving problems and improving processes.

Some companies have found that talking about these myths and misconceptions as they consider working toward ISO registration is an effective way to make sure organizational members understand ISO's key ideas and approaches.

Part II

This part of the book contains 20 chapters, each of which examines one section of the ISO 9001 standard. Each chapter includes the following:

- Several questions to help you focus on the basic issues and concerns found in the section
- An interpretation of the requirements in the section. This interpretation applies to all types and sizes of organizations. It identifies requirements and records that must be established and maintained in order to have a successful ISO 9000 program
- A specific interpretation and application of the section to service organizations
- Several examples that demonstrate how a service provider might interpret and apply the language in the section
- Practical suggestions service practitioners may use to apply the requirements in their service company
- A service organization case study that reports how one ISO registered service company applied the particular section to their operation to become registered
- Finally, in the Lessons Learned discussion, we report the ISO-registered service company's input to the question "What advice would you offer a service company undertaking a registration project?"

5

~❧ ❧~

Section 4.1,
Management Responsibility

THE KEY QUESTIONS

Section 4.1, Management Responsibility, asks:

1. Has management established its strategic vision and does everyone in the company understand the vision?
2. Is management successfully using its quality management system to achieve its strategic objectives?

INTERPRETING THE STANDARD

The first two sections of the standard, Section 4.1, Management Responsibility, and Section 4.2, Quality System, require a service company to identify or to establish its strategic mission and direction. In addition to the vision, management must identify specific strategic objectives for its company. Specifically, Section 4.1 requires senior management to the following:

- Define and document a quality policy and objectives to meet its needs and the expectations of its customers
- Make sure the policy is known and implemented throughout the organization
- Document responsibilities and authorities they expect employees to implement, particularly the authority to prevent nonconformances
- Provide adequate resources to manage the company

- Appoint a Management Representative—from the management group—to be responsible for the ISO program
- Routinely review the quality system and assess its continuing suitability to satisfy the company's and customers' needs

Interestingly enough, neither Section 4.1, Management Responsibility, nor 4.2, Quality System, requires your service company to write a procedure that describes how you satisfy the requirements of these two sections. Instead, a description of how you do this usually is included as part of your quality manual.

SERVICE PERSPECTIVES ON MANAGEMENT RESPONSIBILITY

The first of the 20 sections of the ISO standard requires your company to establish and articulate your strategic mission and objectives. ISO is a *management* initiative rather than a *quality* initiative, and this section of the standard requires senior management to connect the ISO registration process to the global direction of the corporation. Just as a manufacturing organization must determine its products, markets, and customers, your service organization also must define itself in the marketplace. The chief executive officer, as "supplier's management with executive responsibility," in the words of the standard, with the support of his or her staff, must set and articulate the overall direction of the organization.

Several key ideas in the ISO standards revolve around definitions. The standards use the term *supplier* throughout to refer to the company that seeks and becomes registered to one of the ISO 9000 standards. The term *executive responsibility* identifies the highest-ranking individual within the organization as defined by the scope of its ISO registration. The scope can be any defined organization, such as a loan-servicing company, or a self-contained unit within an organization, such as the training division of a credit-card company. It can also purposely exclude certain groups and functions within the organization. Companies determine the scope of their registration in concert with their registrar. The highest-ranking person within the defined scope of the registration may be a department head if the department is separately registered.

A *nonconformance* is any action or omission that fails to satisfy one of the requirements of the standard. A nonconformance could be a failure to address one of the requirements in the standard, or it could be a failure to follow through and act on established procedures or work instructions. *Requirements* can be established by the ISO standard, any regulatory body, your own company practices, or they can be something your customer expects you to do.

Executive Responsibilities

There are five subclauses in this section of the standard. The first subclause of this section charges the CEO or executive with four primary responsibilities. They are to:

- Define the quality policy
- Establish the strategic objectives for the organization
- Articulate a commitment to quality
- Ensure that everyone throughout the organization understands and adheres to the quality policy

The requirement in this section to establish the objectives for quality connects the idea of quality with the idea of making a profit for the business. The equivalent goal for not-for-profit companies is to sustain the organization and use its resources effectively. According to ISO, companies that successfully implement a quality policy are rewarded with financial or operating success.

Most companies bring to an ISO implementation project already established strategic plans and related goals for the short, medium, and long term. Where these strategies have not been articulated, the ISO registration project offers an additional benefit because it is far easier to reach organizational success when these objectives have been defined.

The ISO quality system must clearly support your company's quest to meet its strategic goals. ISO is not a separate activity. It must be an integral part of daily operations and must help and support the company's achievement of its strategic objectives. Management can demonstrate that the ISO program is an integral part of their daily operations by assuring that everyone throughout the organization understands and adheres to the quality policy.

The concept of making a profit is further supported by the standard in the quality policy, which must support your organizational goals and expectations and focus on the needs of your customers. Determining customer needs and expectations is critical to setting the strategic direction of the company. There is a clear assumption you have invested in appropriate customer feedback or market research, whether this is through formal surveys, through talking to your customers, or any other tactics you use to learn customer needs. The ISO standard supports the need for an organizational framework and structure to help your service company focus its efforts to achieve your strategic goals and objectives. A metric and a time-frame should be identified for each of the organization's strategic goals to measure progress toward meeting them.

Responsibilities and Authorities of Employees

The second subclause of this section requires you to define responsibilities and authorities for your employees and associates. In particular, it asks you to establish how able they are to support achievement of your quality goals. Authorities and responsibilities can be spelled out in a number of different ways. Typically, authorities and responsibilities are included in:

- Procedures and work instructions
- Organizational charts
- Job descriptions
- Performance assessments, including plans for employee development
- Training and/or experience requirements

ISO does not specifically require your company to use any of these items. Many alternative ways can help you meet the requirement. However, you must address the requirement in a coherent way that satisfies your own internal operational needs and helps your company satisfy your customers. One of the real challenges of ISO, then, is figuring out the best way to do things to meet your own needs. ISO does not tell you how to do anything, only what issues you must address.

In addition to defining responsibilities and authorities, the standard also requires your company to establish the interrelationship among people and among organizational groups. The standard does not permit finger-pointing and requires all parts of your organization to function as a coherent unit. One of the primary outcomes of ISO registration is focusing everyone in the organization

on satisfying customers—including internal customers—and helping your company achieve its goals. Most service organizations
intuitively understand the need to satisfy customers, and in some
ways they have an easier time with this concept than do manufacturing organizations, which tend to be more process- and machine-
oriented than customer-oriented.

Your registrar's auditors will be particularly interested in looking
at the interrelationships among your groups and functions. Cooperation and clean hand-offs are expected; throwing a problem "over
the wall to the next cubicle" is definitely not acceptable.

This second subclause of the section focuses particularly on making sure individuals have organizational authority to identify and
fix problems. ISO does not use the term *continuous improvement*.
However, the idea is prevalent throughout the various sections of
the standard, particularly in Corrective and Preventive Action (Section 4.14).

Responsibilities and authorities must be clearly defined for those
individuals who have the organizational freedom to identify problems, report them, seek solutions, initiate solutions, and to follow
up to make sure solutions are effective. Most important, individuals must have the authority to ensure that nonconformances are not
allowed to slip through the system and on to the customer.

This subclause of the standard also establishes a basic theme that
reappears in the section on Internal Quality Audits (Section 4.17)
and Control of Nonconforming Product (Section 4.13). Essentially,
all three sections encourage your service company to establish a
disciplined problem-solving process to create and cultivate an environment in which employees know they can and must identify
problems and opportunities for improvement. Further, this environment should support employees' efforts to seek out the causes,
not just the symptoms, of problems.

Infrastructure

The last three subclauses of this section require your company to
establish an infrastructure to support the ISO quality assurance and
management initiative. The standard specifically requires your service company to obtain and assign sufficient resources to support
the work and tasks necessary to satisfy customers. Resources

include physical and human capital, including time and people, as well as equipment. Most manufacturing settings are equipment- and capital-intensive, and many service organizations are people-intensive. In both cases, the standard requires there to be sufficient resources to produce the service and satisfy the customer. One key resource is people who must have adequate experience and training to enable them to do their assigned tasks. As evidence of this focus, this section of the standard specifically identifies training for internal auditors, a theme that will be repeated in Internal Quality Audits (Section 4.17) and Training (Section 4.18).

Management Representative

In the fourth subclause, the individual with executive responsibility must appoint someone from within his or her own management to serve as the ISO Management Representative (MR). Because the MR must be a member of the *supplier's own management*, the MR cannot be a consultant or part-time individual. More importantly, the MR must be someone with sufficient credibility and organizational or positional clout to move the company toward registration. The Management Representative is usually the individual charged with helping the company organize the project to achieve registration.

The Management Representative's tasks do not require the position to be a full-time job, and in most small and medium-size companies, the MR tasks are one part of an individual's job. The standard identifies the tasks associated with being an MR as "irrespective of other responsibilities," which means the MR can and probably should have other tasks assigned. In fact, many of the MRs we spoke with see their ISO responsibilities as only one of their set of tasks or responsibilities.

The Management Representative is charged with the overall responsibility for the ISO 9000 quality assurance project. Your MR should work with other individuals within your organization, first, to establish the quality assurance process and, as an ongoing responsibility, to make sure it continues to support your organization's needs. One of the MR's primary responsibilities is to periodically prepare and present an analysis report on the ISO 9000 system for the chief executive.

Periodic Assessment

The final subclause of this section of the standard requires the chief executive to periodically assess the efficacy of the ISO quality assurance process. ISO requires companies to plan a strategic direction with measurable objectives, then to establish tactics and operations to achieve those objectives. The management review process requires your senior executive to assess regularly how well the company is progressing toward meeting its goals. Equally important, the review process helps your company focus on the extent to which the ISO process is supporting your company's achievement of its goals.

The language of the standard says this review should be conducted at *defined intervals*. During the time when you are initiating your ISO project, these intervals should probably be biweekly or monthly. Once registration is achieved, they can be reduced to quarterly or semiannually. It is always appropriate to include an ISO agenda item for routine strategic planning meetings. There is no requirement for the management review to be a meeting. It could be a report presented to the senior manager. Frequently, however, it is more useful to conduct management reviews as a discussion among the senior decision makers. Also, management review does not have to be an undertaking separate from routine strategic planning activities of the company. It can be included as part of any routinely held strategic planning or review meeting.

PRACTICAL EXAMPLES

- To ensure the quality policy *"is understood . . . at all levels of the organization,"* the president of a worldwide engineering consulting firm may appear in a new employee orientation videotape explaining the company's quality goals and vision statement.
- To ensure the *"commitment to quality . . . shall be relevant to the supplier's organizational goals,"* an international sales force may carry business cards with the quality/vision statement printed on the back of the cards in the native language of the country in which they sell their service.
- To ensure the quality commitment is *"relevant to . . . the expecta-*

tions and needs of its customers," a hotel chain may include their commitment to quality on the sign-in form guests complete upon registration.

- To document how personnel *"initiate action to . . . identify and record any problems relating to the . . . process,"* a telemarketing service may establish a flowchart of actions to take when a contacted individual requests to be removed from the company's database.
- To provide *"resource requirements and provide adequate resources,"* the job training for a nursing home attendant may include actions to initiate and whom to contact for a resident in respiratory distress.
- To report *"on the performance of the quality system to . . . management for review and as a basis for improvement,"* a preventive maintenance team may conduct quarterly reviews of shop orders for unscheduled downtime.
- To *"provide . . . verification activities including internal quality audits,"* a franchisee of a sub/sandwich shop may exchange internal auditors with another area franchisee.

COMPLYING WITH SECTION 4.1 IN SERVICE ORGANIZATIONS

Manage Your Management

The initiative to seek and obtain ISO registration might originate with the CEO or at any level within an organization. Regardless, senior management has a basic responsibility to support the program. That does not imply, however, that the CEO has either the time or inclination to learn everything there is to know about ISO and to drive the project from the executive suite. Smart management representatives employ a team-based approach and involve as many individuals as possible in the project. They thoughtfully orchestrate their senior management's involvement in the process. The CEO has a full agenda and will appreciate the direction and support provided by the ISO team.

Define Your Scope of Registration

Your service organization, working in concert with your selected registrar, should define the scope of your registration based on your own needs and your customers' expectations. Usually, a scope of registration is limited to one geographical location or to one coherent group or organization. However, you determine the scope of registration to meet your needs. In fact, one group or function, such as customer support training, or a single division within a company may seek and obtain registration. Sometimes companies make a strategic decision to register one function or one location as a way to learn about ISO and then bring other functions or sites into the scope.

Find Simple Ways to Publicize Your Quality Policy

Generally, your quality policy should be found in a variety of locations and formats. First, it should be included among the first several pages of your quality manual. It is also usually found framed in conspicuous locations around the facility. In an effort to make sure all employees and associates are familiar with the policy, think about printing it on the back of employee business cards, posting it on local bulletin boards, or including it on identification badges or pens, as well as on printed items such as letterheads, advertisements, and company marketing materials. The objective in publicizing your quality policy is to make clear to all your constituents that quality is a dominant part of your company's efforts.

Avoid Hyperbole

Usually, the quality policy is short; a few sentences or a single memorable phrase is typical. Unfortunately, many policies suffer from verbose, grandiose hyperbole. ISO does not require companies to demonstrate superior quality, and registration is not an indication your company has achieved world-class stature as a result of your quality program. ISO registration recognizes that your company has achieved a basic, well-organized management system. Therefore, a simple quality policy with no more than four or five items is sufficient to satisfy the requirements of this section of the standard. Essentially, the policy should include your company's intentions in the following areas:

- Valuing customers and providing an excellent service to them
- Valuing employees, making a good organization to work for
- Adhering to the requirements of the ISO 9001 (or 9002) standard

- Making a profit and being successful; or for not-for-profits, sustaining the organization and using our resources appropriately

Most companies with knowledge of or experience in quality practice understand the first two elements of the quality policy. They are a basic characteristic of virtually all quality programs and employee involvement initiatives. Companies registered to one of the ISO standards should obviously adhere to the third item in the list. The final idea may seem obvious. However, if the ISO 9000 registration does not help your service company make a profit and grow the business, then the registration effort may be an expensive and perhaps valueless exercise.

Avoid Counting How Many Angels Can Dance on the Head of a Pin

In several locations in the standard, the writers have added some language that tends to cause confusion. The first of these is in Section 4.1.2.1, which says you must define duties and responsibilities for work *"affecting quality."* This phrase seems to suggest that some individuals do work that does not affect quality. Registrar auditors, as well as management and quality practitioners, understand that every individual and every task *affects quality*. Attempts to delineate exceptions lead to obtuse and arcane philosophical discussions—akin to counting how many angels can dance on the head of a pin. In fact, efforts to eliminate any individual or task from the ISO quality program typically are more difficult than including them. There is more discussion on this topic and suggestions on how to overcome these difficulties in Chapter 6 on Quality System (Section 4.2) and Chapter 9 on Document and Data Control (Section 4.5).

CASE STUDIES AND LESSONS LEARNED

Remaining chapters of this book include a case study that describes, first, how one service company applied the requirements of the section of the standard discussed in that chapter and, second, the lessons they learned along the way. Throughout the process of gathering information for these case studies, several recurring themes emerged. These six recurring themes apply to all sections of the standard and to all companies interviewed.

ISO Isn't Rocket Science

ISO is a very basic, commonsense-based series of requirements. It is not complicated. Unfortunately, because ISO developed in manufacturing settings, service organizations may be intimidated by its language and terminology and not see clearly at first how to interpret and apply it to their own processes. In addition, on its surface, it appears mechanistic and formulaic. Despite this initial impression, however, its ideas are accessible and applicable. Fortunately, as more service companies, registrars, and consultants gain experience with ISO, these interpretation and application problems are diminishing.

Forget Quality, Think Management

ISO 9000 is not a *quality* system. It is a *management* system. In fact, it would be possible to eliminate the word *quality* from the standard and substitute *management* and have a very good idea of what the standard requires. The fundamental ideas learned in Management 101 apply to the basics of ISO.

Forget the Standard, Think Customers

No one should ever be able to say that he or she is doing something extraordinary to satisfy the ISO standard. There are requirements to be met, and you must address each and every one of them in order to become registered. The primary requirement is to satisfy the customer, not the standard. ISO argues that a key element of customer satisfaction is controlling internal processes and avoiding errors and waste (nonconformances). The basic organizational goal of reducing costs is met in large measure by eliminating waste. In the end, an organization's real costs are not those related to quality but those related to lack of quality. If a plan or a procedure or an activity does not contribute to meeting the organization's goals, it is not in the spirit of ISO.

Involve Everyone

ISO is not separate from everyone's daily work life. Employees do not "do quality," they do work. ISO is part of the work. One way to gain buy-in from everyone is to involve as many people in the process as early as possible.

Plan, Do, Check, Act

All the requirements in the ISO standard form a coherent whole and are based on the Shewhart Cycle to "Say what you do, Do what you say, Check the differences, and Act or adjust to fix the problems." The ISO standard was cobbled together by an international committee working from a variety of documents and perspectives, giving rise to initial challenges in reading and interpretation. Because it must satisfy an international community and undergo revisions every five years, this is not likely to change. As service practitioners gain experience working with, interpreting, and applying the standard, however, these difficulties diminish and the standard becomes more comfortable to work with.

ISO Is Not a Magic Bullet

A lot of quality initiatives and short-lived, consultant-generated miracle promises have been foisted on management and employees over the years. ISO is not an ultimate solution or recipe. It is a guide to good management. It will not solve all problems or make the world a perfect place free of errors and frustrations. Rather, it provides a framework within which employees can understand expectations and uses structures to meet organizational objectives.

LESSONS LEARNED

Throughout the book, each chapter concludes with a section on lessons learned about that particular section of the standard. The one overarching and continuing theme among all the lessons is that ISO is both achievable and of proven value to organizations. The following chapters and their case studies will illustrate this argument vividly. Although a challenging road, it is one that leads service companies to important and powerful outcomes.

6

⁓⛥⛥⁓

Section 4.2,
Quality System

THE KEY QUESTIONS

Section 4.2, Quality System, asks:

1. Is management effectively using a quality system that meets the requirements of its customers, its employees, and the ISO 9000 standard?
2. Does the quality system provide a way to "Say what you do, Do what you say, Check the differences, and Act to correct the differences?"

INTERPRETING THE STANDARD

The section on Quality System (Section 4.2), along with Management Responsibility (Section 4.1), requires the company to articulate the strategic mission and structure of the management system. That is, this section requires the service company to establish the framework within which the ISO quality management structure operates. In ISO language, the *system* is "a means of ensuring that product conforms" to customer requirements. Specifically, this section requires your service company to develop:

- A quality manual covering the requirements of the standard
- Procedures required by the standard
- Plans that document your methods of operation

Most importantly, this section of the standard requires you to "effectively implement the quality system and its documented procedures." Not only must you say what you do, but you must also do what you say. The fundamental idea is consistent with the Shewhart Cycle—Say, Do, Check, Act.

SERVICE PERSPECTIVES ON QUALITY SYSTEM

The concern that organizations "say what they do and do what they say" underlies all 20 sections of the ISO 9000 standard. Your documentation system, quality manual, procedures, and plans represent the method used to "say what you do."

ISO requires your service company to describe and explain how you meet each of the requirements in the standard. You do this in the form of 138 *shalls*, or requirements in the standard. For example, among others, you *shall* maintain records of your management review meetings (Section 4.1.3), you *shall* maintain records of your contract review process (Section 4.3.4), and you *shall* maintain training records (Section 4.18). The ISO 9001 standard requires you to maintain a minimum of 18 kinds of records, and 18 procedures. ISO 9002 does not include Design Control (Section 4.4), so the numbers for it are 119 shalls, 17 procedures, and 16 records.

Service organizations face several challenges when they approach the ISO documentation requirements. In contrast to manufacturing organizations that have little difficulty describing their physical systems, frequently the service process is based on human interaction, and much of the service activity is personal, that is it arises out of a specific interaction between an individual and a customer. That does not mean service persons do not work within established frameworks that can be described, however. The challenge is to create documentation to accurately describe what you do and that is used by employees to help them successfully do their work.

It can be useful to think of documentation for ISO as a four-level pyramid. The top piece of the pyramid is the quality manual, the next level contains procedures and plans, the next contains individual work instructions, and the bottom level contains the records generated as evidence that activities addressing the top layers of the pyramid have been met.

A typical quality manual is 40 to 70 pages long and includes a brief description of the company and its services. It then addresses how the service organization meets each of the requirements in each of the 20 sections of the standard. Usually, companies address each section of the standard in one section of the quality manual, and although this is not required, they use a section numbering system to mirror the ISO standard numbering. The manual also must include an outline or description of your company's documentation structure. You can present this either in Quality System (Section of 4.2) or in Document and Data Control (Section 4.5). Because you must address each section and requirement of the standard, it is frequently easier to describe the structure of the documents in Section 4.2 and the way they are developed and maintained in Section 4.5.

The second tier of the documentation pyramid includes procedures and plans. The requirement to include plans is new to the 1994 version of the standard, and there remains some confusion in the difference between plans and procedures. As a rule-of-thumb, a *procedure* describes a process and is routinely used in operations. A *plan* may contain similar elements, such as activities and tasks, responsibilities and authorities, related documents and other categories of information, but in addition, plans include milestones to drive particular activities. Procedures describe organizational functions and major activities. Plans describe projects. Procedures are usually function-specific whereas plans are project-, customer-, or activity-specific. For example, a procedure might describe how you organize a specific customer service activity whereas a plan may describe how you intend to carry out the activity to service one customer. Sometimes the differences are a toss-up, and you should simply decide which is which for your own purposes. In either case, avoid redundancy. It is unnecessary to have both plans and procedures to describe the same activities.

A significant challenge facing both manufacturing and service organizations—as well as registrar auditors—is to determine what procedures and plans are necessary and to what level of detail they need to be written. The standard says, "the range and detail of the procedures . . . shall be dependent upon the complexity of the work, the methods used, and the skills and training needed by personnel involved in carrying out the activity." This definition leaves wide latitude for interpretation. Registrars and auditors frequently struggle to assess what procedures are needed and how detailed the pro-

cedures need to be. Service companies and manufacturing companies also typically have difficulty trying to understand exactly how
best to meet these requirements. When trying to assess the need for
a particular procedure and the amount of detail, a few commonsense rules-of-thumb apply:

- If employees don't use it, it is unnecessary
- If high risk, either financial or personal, is related to the activity, you need one
- If it is critical that something be done in a certain way, or in a
  certain order, you need one
- If the tasks are complex or infrequently performed, you need
  one
- If there is high employee turnover or limited resources to train
  employees, you need one
- If people simply feel more comfortable having one, you need
  one

One of the things you do not want to do is play "what if" games.
What if games include developing a procedure describing what
would happen if three purchasing clerks were lost in a freak acci-
dent. What if there was a major flood and everything was washed
away? What if "Joe" became angry and walked off the job? Every
company needs to do succession and resource planning, and they
need to assess the risks inherent in change. They do not, however,
need to plan for and document every possible contingency as part
of their quality program. Trying to document every activity or what
you would do in every possible situation will surely result in frustration; and it will be a waste of time. ISO does not require you to
document the world of possibilities.

Even with these rules-of-thumb, you are going to face difficulties
trying to decide what procedures to write and how detailed they
need to be. Since the standard's inception in 1987, registrars around
the world routinely report that most nonconformances written
against companies during audits are related to documentation,
either against Quality System (Section 4.2) because the documentation is insufficient, or against Document and Data Control (Section
4.5) because the physical control of documentation is faulty.

At the third level of the pyramid are work instructions and forms.
Work instructions generally consist of one page covering one task

performed by one or two persons that can be done in a short time. Checklists, flowcharts, look-up tables, diagrams, forms, labels, and maps are only a few of a wide variety of job aids that serve effectively as work instructions. Work instructions are sometimes called job aids.

Finally, the fourth level of the documentation pyramid are records. The standard requires you to maintain 18 types of records. The standard specifically refers to *quality records*. However, this is another one of those language or terminology issues that sometimes confuses practitioners. There really is no such thing as a quality record. Any paper or computer-generated record used to operate your business that is evidence something happened should be considered a record and must be controlled under the requirements of Control of Quality Records (Section 4.16). Records are evidence something happened. In ISO jargon, records are *"objective evidence"* that you are following your quality management system.

It is important to distinguish between a document and a record because the standard establishes different requirements for how you handle each. A blank form is a document. For example, an expense form for a sales representative is a document. A blank airline ticket is a document. Your company letterhead stationery is a document. However, once the document is used to chronicle an event, that used document then becomes a record.

PRACTICAL EXAMPLES

- To *"prepare a quality manual covering the requirements of this International Standard,"* an advertising/marketing firm may produce an ISO quality manual that demonstrates their design capability and is used to market their services.
- To *"prepare documented procedures consistent with the requirements of this International Standard,"* a multinational bank may include all of their operating procedures and work instructions on their worldwide intranet.
- To *"effectively implement the quality system and its documented procedures,"* the training function within a regional telephone company may produce job aids and work instructions as part of their training program.
- To *"define and document how the requirements for quality"* plan-

ning will be met, a test laboratory may use a scheduling database program to plan and control work flows.

- To ensure adequate *"preparation of quality plans,"* the authors of a book on ISO in service organizations may use a one-page matrix of chapters to topics within the chapters to plan the writing work.

COMPLYING WITH SECTION 4.2 IN SERVICE ORGANIZATIONS

Identify the "Shalls"

Review the standard and highlight each *shall*. Make sure you have 138 of them. Also highlight each location where the standard includes this reference: *(See 4.16)*. That parenthetical expression means you must keep a record for that activity. You must also have at least one procedure for each section of the standard from Section 4.3 through 4.20. With your list of *shalls*, records, and procedures in hand, you have the beginning of a list of things you need to become registered to ISO and are now ready to begin to conduct your gap assessment.

Conduct a Gap Assessment

A gap assessment is a base-line audit that identifies your current level of compliance with the requirements of the standard. More simply, a gap assessment asks, "What do we have and what do we need?" Most companies quickly discover that there are many processes in place and initiatives underway to support the requirements of ISO 9000. The assessment will identify initiatives and systems you can use or which you can modify or update to satisfy the requirements. It will also identify missing pieces you need to develop. The gap assessment will serve as a basic planning document as you develop your ISO implementation project plan.

Begin Your Plan

Achieving ISO registration, like any other project or process your company engages in, requires planning and resources. You may decide to use computer-based project management software, but this is not required. You will need to establish some effective way to plan resources, tasks, timelines, milestones, and ways to assess achievement.

Don't Let the Word "Quality" Complicate Decisions

The standard refers to a quality manual and quality procedures and plans. Similarly, Section 4.16 refers to quality records. Every procedure, plan, and record is part of your quality system. It is asking for trouble to try to distinguish between documents and records that deal with quality and those that do not. Such distinctions are usually a waste of time. Begin this part of the process with the attitude that your service company is a quality organization and everything it does is about quality, including all of its documents and records.

Write Your Quality Manual Last

Many companies make the strategic and political mistake of trying to write their quality manual first. Like ISO registration itself, writing the quality manual is a politically charged undertaking. You are much better off first developing procedures, work instructions, and plans. Once those documents are in place and everyone gains experience working with your established ISO system and its documentation, it is then possible to spend a few hours summarizing your system as you write your quality manual.

Trying to write a manual first usually becomes an exercise in wishes and dreams. It is unlikely at the outset managers and employees will understand the system or their responsibilities within it. Fear can raise political barriers and create dissent, delaying your registration by six months or more as you fight the inevitable political battles. You do not need your quality manual until just before you become registered. Put the system in place and refine it first. Then write and distribute the quality manual for approval. Using this approach, employees and managers will recognize the quality manual as a description of the existing system and willingly embrace it, and you will sidestep a potential political nightmare.

One alternative to the strategy of writing your quality manual last is to begin drafting it as part of the gap assessment and project planning process to help identify areas to address and tasks to accomplish. If you adopt this strategy, be sure to keep the quality manual within the implementation team as a draft or planning document. If you must reveal parts of it to anyone outside the team, be sure to identify it for what it is—a planning tool.

CASE STUDY IN QUALITY SYSTEM

The core business of Technical and Further Education (TAFE) is providing training in the vocational education sector throughout Australia. TAFE Queensland, with a full-time equivalency staff of 8,000, consists of 16 institutes similar to community colleges in the United States. They provide vocational education and training throughout the state of Queensland and some other areas of Australia, as well as to some international markets, particularly in Asia. Queensland, one of six states in Australia, is located in the northeast quadrant of the continent. It covers 1.7 million square kilometers and has a population of some 3.4 million.

In 1996, the Australia National Training Authority (ANTA), a primary funding body for tertiary education in Australia, decreed that to receive funds, training organizations must have a quality management system in place. In addition, the purchasing policy of the State Government of Queensland stipulated that any organization tendering or asking for state government funds after January 1, 1996, would be required to have at least second-party quality assurance certification. TAFE Queensland decided to become registered to ISO 9000 as part of their way to satisfy these mandated requirements. Another primary advantage for seeking ISO registration was having an external assessment of their training programs recognized in the international business community. Because a major component process in educational organizations is the design of curriculum, they elected to become registered to the 9001 standard because of its inclusion of Design Control (Section 4.4).

Interestingly enough, they took on their ISO registration project in the middle of a massive restructuring effort to combine 32 state colleges into 16 institutes. TAFE Queensland was the first state educational body to attempt ISO registration, so they had few opportunities to benchmark or learn from others. As important, although each institute had help and encouragement from the central state TAFE staff, each undertook its own registration project independently.

Three members of the ISO registration effort described the process they used to accomplish registration. Sheridan van Asch was the Senior Executive Officer of the TAFE Queensland Organisational Development Directorate. Her responsibilities were to link the ISO project to the broader quality agenda set by the Australian Quality Council. Alex McGill was the TAFE Quality Manager responsible for supporting all 16 institutes to achieve ISO registration. Andrea Harris is the Quality Manager at one of the institutes, the Gold Coast Institute of TAFE.

The process developed by the Gold Coast Institute of TAFE to introduce ISO reflects the process used by the majority of institutes. The Quality Managers from all the Institutes created a Quality Network to ensure they provided each other with support and a forum in which to share their processes for implementing ISO.

Andrea and the staff at Gold Coast did several things to address the particular needs and concerns of their organization. First, they determined that the language in the ISO standard had little relevance to the world-view of the average institute staff member. Additionally, they thought the manufacturing-oriented concepts would be off-putting to their staff. Therefore, rather than get bogged down in trying to teach all their staff members to interpret the standard, they focused on its intent and outcomes, its salient features, benefits, and—most importantly—how the program would directly affect individual members of the staff. In particular, they were concerned about the need for procedures, feedback mechanisms, and document control.

Rather than teaching members about the ISO standard, they focused their training effort on teaching staff how to write procedures and provided general guidance and support—along with a format template—and asked individuals to describe what they did and how. The basic guidance they gave the staff was that if it is an important task and someone needed to step in tomorrow and could not figure out what or how to do it, then write a procedure. According to Andrea, the first problem the staff faced was the tendency to overwrite individual procedures and to write too many procedures. As they gained a clearer understanding of the purposes for the procedures and desired outcomes, however, they were able to learn to adjust both the amount of detail and the number of individual procedures to provide a reasonable picture of the staff's activities.

As the staff worked on the procedure development project, it became obvious to the core team that many of the requirements of the standard were in place and being met. In some other instances, adjustments to processes and subsequent documentation of them adequately satisfied the requirements. Some requirements were not being met, however, and there was no process in place to meet them, so the core team built and implemented processes to help the institute meet its needs, satisfy its customers, and meet the requirements of the ISO standard. Interestingly, all of these changes were seen by the institute's staff as valuable improvements to their processes.

There were several benefits to the approach adopted by Gold Coast and several of the other TAFE Queensland institutes. According to Alex McGill, TAFE Quality Manager, in those institutes that did not focus on the details of the standard, there was less confusion about the purpose of seeking registration and less resistance to the ISO implementation project. In those institutes where staff members were asked to write procedures describing their own tasks, the members took pride in ownership and more willingly adopted the procedures as valuable. In contrast, in those institutes that decided to have the core team write procedures to describe other staff members' jobs, there was more resistance to adopting the procedures and a common view that the procedures were not helpful.

Alex and Sheridan knew the Gold Coast Institute has always had a strong customer focus, so there was no need for a fundamental cultural shift. Staff and management view students, community, employers, and industry as their customers. They also have a strong commitment to each other as internal customers. The ISO registration process, along with their reengineering program, helped them bring consistency to the service they offer to their customers. The program gave them a basic set of guides to control processes, train new staff, and to help current staff learn new skills and tasks. A common set of processes and multiskilled staff have heightened confidence, enhanced communication, allowed flexibility, and at the same time brought consistency to their service.

LESSONS LEARNED

A primary outcome of the ISO registration process at TAFE is the staff has been able to focus on the practical importance and outcomes of a quality program. This is evidenced by an approach that looks at systems rather than at people as the source of problems. It has allowed the staff to focus on deficiencies within the system rather than on the individuals involved. This shift in perspective, in effect, has become a license for staff to be comfortable reporting deficiencies and identifying opportunities for improvement. Further, this approach has allowed the institute to:

- Seek feedback from customers about issues important to the customer
- Use customer issues as self-assessment performance indicators
- Establish benchmarks and set objectives for customer satisfaction

The ISO 9000 process enabled many of the institutes to broaden their view and understanding of business improvement processes. It provided many of them with a good basis upon which to move to implementing a broader quality agenda. This resulted in the Southbank Institute of TAFE winning a High Commendation at the Australian Quality Council Awards in 1997.

In total the reengineering process, along with their ISO registration process, allowed the TAFE Queensland institutes to transform themselves based on organizational and customer needs by involving many staff members in the projects.

7

~✦ ✦~

Section 4.3, Contract Review

THE KEY QUESTIONS

Section 4.3, Contract Review, asks:

1. Do we understand what our customer wants?
2. Have we agreed with the customer what is needed?
3. Can we deliver—do we have the capability to deliver—the service our customer wants?

INTERPRETING THE STANDARD

The basic principle underlying the ISO standard is to satisfy the customer. In Section 1.0, the standard says, "The requirements . . . are aimed primarily at achieving customer satisfaction . . ." Section 4.3, Contract Review, requires the service company to ask itself three questions: "Do we understand what our customer wants?"; "Do we and the customer agree on what we are to deliver?"; and "Can we deliver the service?" Note that Contract Review focuses on your delivery of service to customers. Contracts with your own vendors and subcontractors are covered under Purchasing (Section 4.6).

In addition to a procedure that describes how your company reviews and approves contracts and a record that the review has been completed, the standard requires that:

- Contracts be reviewed to make sure customer requirements are clearly defined

- Differences between what the customer ordered and what you are able to deliver are resolved
- Your company has the capability to meet the requirements
- You specify how amendments to contracts are made
- Interested/affected persons within your organization are notified of changes to the contract

This section of the standard allows you to use verbal agreements in addition to written agreements to receive, accept, and approve a contract or *tender*—a tender is an ISO term for a request from a customer for a bid—as long as there is a process in place to make sure the order is accurate and agreed upon.

SERVICE PERSPECTIVES ON CONTRACT REVIEW

Contract Review (Section 4.3) and Purchasing (Section 4.6) ask your service company to focus on similar core issues. Contract Review defines your relationship with your customer, whereas Purchasing defines your relationship with your vendors and subcontractors. A major difference is that Contract Review allows you to conduct business on a verbal or written basis, whereas the Purchasing section requires documentation and does not include that flexibility.

Finding out what customers want is a continuing challenge. Contract Review expects you to define what it is you will provide or sell to your customers and then describe that service clearly and accurately to them. From a practical, strategic perspective, it is necessary but not sufficient to define the features of your service. You must discover what features customers believe are important and see as value-added. Woe be to the company that has a wonderful service and grand features customers do not care about. Such a company will go broke because people will not buy. Moreover, as customers become accustomed to improved quality service throughout their business dealings, they have less patience with substandard performance. In fact, excellent service is becoming standard and expected. Service organizations intuitively should have an easier time than manufacturing companies in dealing with Contract Review. Many people in your service company have direct contact with your customers, and you receive fairly quick feedback if there is a variance between what is expected and what is delivered.

Contract Review applies to internal customers and across functional groups as well as to external customers. Managing Contract Review with internal customers is often a greater challenge than applying it to external customers, for both service and manufacturing companies. Clearly defining what is expected or ordered between internal functions and how well what is delivered meets expectations and needs among your internal customers may be a critical element of delivering quality to your end customers.

A smoothly efficient ISO management assurance process allows internal groups to see each other as customers and to focus together on the external customer's needs. The overarching program does not allow finger pointing or a "not-my-problem" attitude.

ISO practitioners recognize the implications and importance of satisfying internal customers. A favorite ISO registrar audit practice is to trace a purchase order or tender from the offer or sale through to delivery to the customer. Such auditing techniques quickly identify problems with hand-offs between groups and functions. These frequently reflect breakdowns in communication, which further reflect Contract Review problems between internal customers.

One of the greatest challenges for service practitioners is that services are not always tangible, so it may be difficult to articulate or measure some of the most critical characteristics your customers require and expect. In addition to quantitative features—such as accuracy and timeliness—which can be measured, customers want and expect qualitative features as well. For example, friendliness, security, and trust may be value-added features your customers expect. These are difficult for customers to articulate and for you to measure. Impressions, for example, are important in many situations. For example, if an automotive service area is clean, orderly and not overly noisy, customers may interpret this as evidence service personnel are competent. If the line at the bank is long—regardless of how many tellers are working or how fast the line is moving—customers may develop an impression of poor service. Not only must you offer excellent service, but you also must look like you are offering excellent service. For example, if several persons working behind the counter at an airline check-in desk are working on tasks unrelated to checking in customers while many customers are waiting on line, these customers perceive an unintended message that they are not important and airline personnel are not interested in their needs. Such qualitative and impression management factors are critical to service organization success.

The challenge for your service company is to systematically determine what features customers want and value and to find ways to describe your service to them. Then, it is important to find practical, valid, and reliable ways to measure your performance in providing them. Finding how they perceive your company also allows you to make adjustments in the services you provide and how you frame them to current and potential customers.

PRACTICAL EXAMPLES

- To ensure that they have *"the capability to meet the contract or accepted order requirements,"* a property management firm may review the terms of their agreement for frequency of preventive maintenance schedules with the owners of an office building.
- To ensure that contract requirements *"are adequately defined and documented,"* a house cleaning service may review and approve a local newspaper advertisement listing their various cleaning services and the costs of the individual services.
- To resolve *"any differences between the contract or accepted order requirements,"* a hotel room clerk may ask a guest to review and initial the cost of the room and the check-out time on the guest register form when the guest checks in.

COMPLYING WITH SECTION 4.3 IN SERVICE ORGANIZATIONS

Define, Measure, and Improve Your Service

Contract Review requires you to carefully define what you are doing to provide for your customers. A tender is an offer to sell. It can be a formal written proposal or an advertisement in a newspaper. Both of these tell your customers about your service and promise to satisfy their expectations. Once you decide and agree on which features are important, put metric techniques in place to help determine and demonstrate you are achieving your objectives. There is a direct link between defining the service and measuring your success (see Section 4.20, Statistical Techniques). The measures you establish also will support your continuous improvement program.

Define Your Customers

Everybody is somebody's customer. In addition to the buyers of your services, you have important internal customers. These internal customers include team members, other departments, groups or functions within a location or organization, and divisions with a company spread around the world. Contract Review requires you to open and maintain clear lines of communication and feedback among all internal customers. Many ISO organizational failures are breakdowns in communication among internal customers, not with external customers.

For service organizations, communicating with external customers is a function of more than just the marketing or sales function. While remembering this, do not fall into the common misconception that your sales and marketing persons are not integral to your ISO effort because they are not "inside" employees. They, just like all other members of the organization, have a quality function. The information they provide about customer needs and perceptions is invaluable. In the same way, they must apply quality practices to making the sale, just as the other members do to support the sale.

CASE STUDY IN CONTRACT REVIEW

Dittler Brothers, Inc. in Oakwood, Georgia, designs and manufactures lottery games and tickets for state-run lotteries in the United States as well as in several international markets, including Russia. Even though they manufacture a product—lottery games and tickets—their registration is considered under the service category of Standard Industrial Classification (SIC Code) 2700, and the scope of their ISO 9001 registration is as a service company. Their 350 employees include those who produce the lottery games and tickets, as well as individuals in sales and marketing, legal, and administrative functions. A study of their operations quickly confirms they are indeed a service organization.

Dittler sought ISO registration as part of their growth into international markets. Before seeking registration, they had a very strong quality initiative and internal auditing process. The nature of their business and the monies involved in lottery games and operations require strict control to prevent errors within their own operations or opportunities for fraud by an external agency or person. Joe McMillan, Peggy Coltrane, Shellee Wadsworth, and Mark Janifer led their registration implementation project along with eight internal auditors, about 30 area coordinators from manufacturing and support groups, a documentation team, and a management team. In total, they had about 50 individuals actively working on the project and a great deal of support from everyone in the organization.

Dittler's approach to Contract Review is interesting as an example both of satisfying the requirements of the individual section of the standard and of demonstrating how this section of the standard ties together with several other sections to help develop a coherent communication system within the organization.

The sales and marketing staff works both with the state lottery commissions and with Dittler's design group to devise innovative and creative individual games. The company has a wide variety of elements that can be combined to create various interesting and attractive designs for the game cards and tickets. The sales force works with a Lottery Ticket Request form (LTR), which contains all existing design options in their Master Options Index. The LTR also has an area to describe additional characteristics and elements the customer wants. The LTR becomes the document of record—thereby satisfying the standard's requirement for a record—of the agreement that defines what the game will look like. It also serves as a communication device to the design group, production department, planning group, legal group, and their internal audit group. Their internal audit group, in this instance, is not their ISO internal auditors, but rather the group that audits the game structure and parameters to make sure the odds of winning are correct and there is no possibility someone could figure out in advance which tickets are winners.

As each of the groups finishes their work, they develop a series of working papers which then are reviewed internally as part of their Design Control process and as part of their Contract Review process with the customer to gain final customer approval. The LTR working papers continue to serve as a communication link to the customer and supports Dittler's ISO requirements for Contract Review. They further serve as a link to the design group and internal audit group as part of the Design Control (Section 4.4) requirements, as part of the production control process (Process Control,

Section 4.9), as a measure for their Inspection and Testing (Section 4.10) and Statistical Techniques (Section 4.20).

LESSONS LEARNED

Because of the sensitive nature of their business and strict regulatory requirements, as well as the need for rigorous control in design and quality, the ISO 9001 requirements were not a radical departure for Dittler. Their ISO team did several particularly smart things as they went about implementing their project. First, they formalized a project plan complete with Gantt charts and milestones. They involved many people with individual tasks to contribute to the development and implementation of their ISO program. And as might be expected from a company whose business is creating interest and attention and the production of games, they found innovative ways to involve everyone in the project. For example, they came up with "Dittler Dollars," which were awarded to employees for contributions to the project, participation in internal audits, or for being able to answer an ISO-related question asked by one of the implementation team members. Employees could redeem their dollars for various prizes. The game was an internal marketing tool for them to involve everyone in the ISO program and to gain buy-in from everyone to support the program. Most importantly, they found a way to link the requirements of the standard, based on their LTR working papers and Contract Review process, that formed a structured communication channel with their customers as well as a coherent internal communication framework for their organization.

8

~⚜ ⚜~

Section 4.4,
Design Control

THE KEY QUESTIONS

Section 4.4, Design Control, asks:

1. Do we have a good way to plan how we design the tasks and steps we must do to perform and to control our service processes?
2. Do we incorporate customer requirements and satisfy legal or statutory codes as part of the design process?
3. Is everyone who is affected—or potentially affected—by our service included in the design of the service?
4. Do we periodically review the design processes and do we run pilot tests to make sure our service will satisfy our customers?

INTERPRETING THE STANDARD

In typical goods-producing organizations, two primary activities are engineering and manufacturing. Design Control (Section 4.4) establishes the requirements for engineering and Process Control (Section 4.9) establishes the requirements for manufacturing. It is important to understand that Design Control does not refer to the actual design documents themselves, such as engineering or architectural drawings and specifications. Rather, it refers to the steps designers and engineers follow and the work they do to devise specifications or to design a new service process. In service organizations, the designers are the individuals who create the processes company employees follow to deliver the service.

There are nine subclauses, as well as requirements for one procedure and two records in this section.

General Requirements

First, there must be a specific plan for each design activity. The standard also calls for companies to make sure participating individuals both are qualified and have adequate resources to perform the design functions. Plans describing how the organization develops designs must be routinely updated as the planning process evolves. The plan must define the organizational and technical interfaces to make sure there is a steady flow of information among all parties affected or potentially affected by the evolving design.

Inputs and Outputs

Inputs, by definition, are any information sources designers use to develop the design. Sources may include requests for proposal specifications, customer descriptions, regulatory—industry, state, or federal—codes and standards, specifications for components and parts, Good Manufacturing Practices (GMPs), commonly accepted engineering practices, and a wealth of other informational sources. One critical input is the customer contract where the customer's requirements are specified.

Outputs are the physical results of the designer's work and include such documents as drawings, specifications, architectural designs, flowcharts, exploded views, and construction diagrams. In service organizations, outputs may include task descriptions, check sheets, flowcharts, forms, or any document that takes service personnel through the process of delivering the service. ISO requires these outputs to include characteristics for safe and proper functioning of the product, as well as instructions for safe handling, required maintenance, storage, and disposal. Finally, the standard requires design documents be reviewed before they are released for implementation.

Verification and Validation

Verification is an evaluation of design before production, based on design documents, whereas *validation* looks at the completed product—or a portion of the completed product. Verification asks the basic questions, "Are these designs satisfactory?" and "Do they meet the needs of both the customer and those individuals who are responsible for building or manufacturing the product or providing the service?" The designs must contain enough information and detail that the production or construction persons can use them to manufacture or build the product or service persons can put the service into operation. ISO requires organizations to keep a record of design verification. A common practice that satisfies this requirement is for the lead engineer to sign off on the documents and designs as an indication they have been verified as correct.

Validation is a product- or service-related issue. Validation asks the basic question, "Does the product/service work?" Engineers sometimes build models or prototypes; they may test components or parts, or conduct a physical test of the final product to make sure that it works as intended. Service personnel run practice or pilots to make sure the service will be provided as intended. ISO also asks that design validation be done in a variety of settings and applications if the product/service is supposed to be used in different places and ways or in different applications/settings.

Review and Changes

Formal reviews must be conducted at established intervals and must include persons from all functions related to or affected by the design. ISO also asks that specialist personnel with expertise be included as needed in these reviews. Design changes simply require the organization to identify, document, review, and approve changes to the designs.

SERVICE PERSPECTIVES ON DESIGN CONTROL

As is clearly evident in the definitions and requirements of this section, ISO appears to be mechanistic. Laid out as a flowchart, however, each one of the nine subclauses represents one of a systematic series of steps to describe a planning process. Service organizations will find the requirements of Design Control straightforward and reasonable since they reflect a useful means to plan work and to assure adequate resources and experienced personnel to do the work. Such a planning process will help your service company operate effectively and efficiently, and communicate expectations and desired outcomes to all your internal members.

Interestingly enough, ISO tells engineers in Design Control they ought to pay attention to what the customer ordered. Service organizations, many of whose members are point-of-contact people directly serving the customer, also must consider this particular admonition as they approach design control. Depending on market conditions and response-time pressures, service planning probably needs to reflect more deliberate flexibility, given the dominant need for quick and effective response to customer needs.

Most of the design output requirements are fairly conventional, and any licensed engineer would consider them as fundamental, routine good practice. In contrast, your service organization might have less experience with and therefore more difficulty with the design output requirements. Because the outcome of service is frequently intangible, it may be difficult to produce a physical design product or document. Rather than focusing first on documents, one way to overcome this difficulty is to describe desired customer outcomes and goals and then develop pictorial representations of the processes—for example, a flowchart or decision tree—or other documentation of the steps needed to get to the desired goals.

Your service organization probably will not have a difficult time doing design verification. It is a simple paperwork exercise to develop a checklist of the established requirements in the design or quality plan and then review and check them off against the design output document. Validation may be time- and resource-intensive, but again, it is unlikely to be difficult for service groups. A pilot program, a testing period, service personnel training, role-plays, or a walkthrough demonstration in-house before rolling out a new service will not only verify the adequacy of the design, but will also help everyone understand how the new service process will operate "in real life."

Design review is probably the smartest requirement in this section of the standard. It helps everyone focus on customer needs and stay on track and schedule to devise the service. It simply says that periodically—throughout the design process—everyone must get together and review not only the design work itself, but also the process of how the design planning is progressing. Review requires designers to ask, as the famous former mayor of New York City, the

Honorable Ed Koch used to inquire, "How'm I doin'?" This review requirement seems particularly pertinent and useful for service organizations, especially in its implied involvement of front-line customer service personnel who will be required to effectively implement the newly designed service.

PRACTICAL EXAMPLES

- To *"prepare plans for each design and development activity,"* a pharmaceutical company may develop a complex design project plan to research and bring a new medicine to market.
- To identify *"design input requirements,"* a home remodeling contractor may identify all of the building, zoning, and local codes as part of a plan to add a room addition to an existing home.
- To conduct design *"verification"* and *"validation"* activities, a national theater company may run several "dress rehearsals off-Broadway" to test a new show.

COMPLYING WITH SECTION 4.4 IN SERVICE ORGANIZATIONS

Define Service Design

At first blush, it might appear that your service organizations should side-step Design Control—and seek registration to ISO 9002, which does not include this requirement. You might select this approach on the basis that you do not perform traditional engineering activities. That would be a mistake. In fact, many service companies have significant design processes in order to find ways to meet customer and changing market needs. Moreover, service organizations typically need to revise continuously and update how they respond to customers' needs based on lessons learned day-by-day in the marketplace.

Your design process or project may be as simple as constructing a new form for a clerk at the copy shop to use to record customer orders, or it may be as complicated as conceiving and designing a completely new information service and building a multimillion dollar company. Regardless of the complexity, a well-conceived and well-executed Design Control process will give you a structure within which to respond to individual customer needs and changing market conditions.

Use Different Plans for Different Situations

There is no requirement for you to have only one way to plan your design efforts. Many companies devise a generic design plan and then develop specific plans depending on varying needs. Design plans may be customer-specific, contract-specific, or product- or service-specific.

Establish Internal Communication Links

Develop an organizational communication process that adheres to the quality concept of *upstream engineering*. Process breakdowns may result from communication failures rather than solely from inefficient work flows. ISO does not allow designers to complete their work in an organizational vacuum and then present the finished design as a *fait accompli*, tossing it over the cubicle to other organizational units to figure out how to execute the design. In *upstream engineering*, everyone participates in the process early and is encouraged to add his or her input. When ISO 9000 auditors look at Design Control, they are interested in the communication connections at all stages between the customer signing the contract and the organization providing the service, as well as in how well the service meets the customer's needs. Design Control is an important link among all of these connections.

Importantly, this section of the standard also gives auditors an opportunity to ask people in various departments about how well they work and cooperate together and communicate to get their work done. On this final point, service organizations may have an easier time than manufacturing organizations in demonstrating their communication links because most service organizations share information to accomplish their goals. While manufacturers focus on process and product, service practitioners focus on process and communication.

Avoid Bureaucracy

A secret to successful Design Control is to have a simple and quick process to encourage people to initiate needed changes in the design or the design planning process. Rather than encumbering or punishing people by making it difficult or impossible to initiate a change through a rigid bureaucracy, find quick and easy ways to change the design process. The language in the standard refers to "design results." Be careful not to misinterpret that to mean only the final output documents. It also refers to the effectiveness and efficiency of the design process.

CASE STUDY IN DESIGN CONTROL

Richard Jones Management Consultants, Inc., (RJMC), is a 20-member consultancy in business and organizational strategic planning in Kingston, Ontario, Canada. RJMC is the first consulting company in Canada to be registered to ISO 9001. They do a wide variety of consulting and training for both short- and long-term projects. The company defines itself as a total quality organization specializing in planning and implementing high-performance systems through the development of business, organizational, and functional excellence. RJMC defines high performance as processes to plan, lead, self-manage, and sustain, and they differentiate this from the traditional management steps of planning, organizing, directing, and controlling. They believe management is responsible for leading and for creating an organizational environment that is supported and sustained. Generally, their client relationships tend to be long-term, and they work to ensure that their customers are satisfied and return for additional services.

In addition to founder Richard Jones, Terry Johnson and Lynn Clyde led the company's effort to achieve ISO registration. Jones related that at first, the team struggled with the issue of how Design Control applied to their work, and they almost decided to be registered to ISO 9002, because it differs from ISO 9001 in not requiring a Design Control section. However, they soon recognized that each of their services is tailored to the specific needs of their individual customers and their response to customers is based on figuring out how best to satisfy those needs.

Although as a consulting firm they routinely do thorough designs for each of their services, the language of the standard offers little specific support for service design, so they initially had difficulty in describing how they were satisfying the standard's requirements. They also were challenged at the outset to help their registrar understand how the company's design function met the requirement described in the standard.

In working through this, they identified a significant difference between design as practiced in manufacturing and design as practiced in service organizations. Jones said this idea may be the most difficult to understand for registrars and auditors whose experience has been in manufacturing environments. The difficulty revolves around the difference between systems and processes. Systems are structures that drive the work in manufacturing processes. In a service organization, the process, which might be thought of as what needs to be accomplished, drives the work. Once the service provider understands what the customer needs and how the process needs to work, it is then possible to construct the process, which—like a structure or system—helps work get done.

In doing a "backward attack" on the design process, service organizations are similar to manufacturing configuration engineers, the folks who lay out the assembly line and figure out how all the parts fit together. They decide first on the finished outcome and then determine the necessary steps and processes to get there. Once they have the outcome and processes under control, then they are able to establish the systems to control the work.

ISO is a linear system that describes how management drives the way work is accomplished. For service organizations, however, the process of how work gets done should drive how the ISO system is set up. There is currently a misunderstanding among many, including some registrars and auditors, who see ISO implementation as a way to drive a process. In fact—particularly in service organizations—the opposite is true. The process should dictate the design and implementation of the system. The real trick in implementing ISO is to see it as needing to fulfill a proactive systemic role that initiates the work, rather than a responsive role. The system is there to facilitate the process, not dictate to it. Once the goal is established, it is possible to design the service to meet the goal. As RJMC demonstrates, service providers who are looking at business processes need to start by focusing on the outcome of what they want for the customer and for the business. Then it is possible to determine the route to get there and put the system in place.

LESSONS LEARNED

RJMC sees ISO as a way to confirm the quality of their own internal processes in addition to demonstrating it to others. Although even their own quality people initially questioned the need for registration, Jones thought they needed ISO to evaluate their day-to-day work. He argued that third-party audits are a way to ensure appropriate processes are in place. Jones further argued that sometimes integrity is one of the most important reasons people trust service providers such as consultants. Third-party assessment allows the service company to maintain a high-quality assurance process to demonstrate both an ongoing commitment to providing high-quality service and the systems to support that commitment. For example, financial audits are done to ensure the integrity of the system, not because people are crooks, but to demonstrate that the financial system is working. It is the same with ISO third-party audits. ISO registration and surveillance audits are a motivator to help you keep your quality system functioning to ensure that you provide excellent service to your clients.

9

❧ ❦

Section 4.5, Document and Data Control

The Key Questions

Section 4.5, Document and Data Control, asks:

1. Do we have procedures, work instructions, and other documents that help us do our work?
2. Are we sure that our procedures accurately describe how we do our work?
3. Are procedures and work instructions available and useful to everyone who needs them and does everyone use them?
4. Do we know that everyone has the up-to-date procedures and work instructions they need?
5. Is the documentation we use reviewed and authorized for use by knowledgeable and responsible persons?

Interpreting the Standard

This section is an extension of Section 4.2, Quality System, which requires companies to develop and use documents to describe how work flows and processes are organized. Each section of the standard, starting with Section 4.3, Contract Review, and ending with Section 4.20, Statistical Techniques, contains the language the "supplier shall establish and maintain documented procedures . . . " of the activities related to that particular section of the standard. This means the service company must have a documented procedure for each section of the 9001 standard from Section 4.3 through 4.20, for a total of at least 18 procedures. (Companies registered to ISO 9002 are not responsible for a procedure for Section 4.4, Design Control). Companies may be able to omit procedures for any section of the standard not relevant to their operation.

Section 4.5, Document and Data Control, sets out the requirements for how the company will generate, handle, and control the documents it uses. The definition of *document* includes the quality manual, plans, procedures, work instructions, and forms. Documents also are defined as items the company uses in the course of its operations that are generated by any agency external to the company, such as government bodies, professional organizations, customers, suppliers, or vendors. Items supplied to the company by an external party, such as product specifications, codes and standards, or any materials employees must use to conduct their daily work activities, also must be controlled.

In addition to controlling documents, this section also requires companies to control both internal data and data received from external sources. These data may include database information, product specifications or information, lists, and any data employees use as input to help them provide their service. Documents and data may be in any form, on paper or computer-based. Regardless of format, the same kinds of controls and safeguards must be in place to meet the requirements of this section of the standard.

It is important to carefully distinguish between documents and records. Essentially, documents or data are something that could be used several times as part of the process or work activity. In contrast, a record is objective evidence an activity took place and was completed. A simple example is a form. A blank form is a document. However, once the form is filled in and used, it becomes a record. The blank form is a document and must meet the requirements of Section 4.5, Document and Data Control, whereas the completed form has become a record of an activity and must meet the requirements of Section 4.16, Control of Quality Records.

In addition to a procedure that meets the requirements of the standard, this section requires the following:

- Documents and data be reviewed "for adequacy" before they are issued

- A master list—or equivalent—containing current revisions be maintained
- The master list be made available to employees to preclude anyone using an outdated or obsolete document
- Pertinent issues of documents are available at work locations where needed
- Invalid or obsolete documents are promptly removed
- Obsolete documents retained for legal or knowledge preservation are marked or identified
- Changes to documents are reviewed and approved by the same function or organization—but not necessarily the same individual(s)—that approved the original
- Reviewers of changed documents have access to information that initiated the change
- The changes are identified in the new document—when practical

Interestingly enough, there is no requirement for any record in this section of the standard. However, as part of the approval processes, someone will usually sign a master copy of the document. That signature then identifies the "record copy" of the document. Further, the standard does not stipulate that you must know where every controlled copy of every document is located. In practice, however, it is impossible to assure that everyone has a current revision of a particular document unless you know where every copy of every document is located.

SERVICE PERSPECTIVES ON DOCUMENT AND DATA CONTROL

One of the keys to ISO documentation is it describes your processes, not only to your registrar auditors, but also to your management and your employees. The documented system helps all parties understand what must be done and how it is done. In this way, documents serve as an important communication device to articulate expectations, responsibilities, and authorities.

The ISO standard requires your service company to have at least 18 procedures (17 if you are registered to ISO 9002), one for each section of the standard from Section 4.3 through Section 4.20. You do not need to write a procedure for a section that does not apply to your company. Each of these procedures describes how you meet the *shalls* of that section. Your job is to establish and follow procedures for each section. These represent the "Say" portion of the PDCA, Shewart Cycle of "Say What You Do, Do What You Say, Check and Fix the Differences."

Some of the most valuable, and frequently unanticipated, outcomes of the ISO documentation process are the system improvements, heightened performance consistency, and consensus building that result as individuals work together to develop procedures for their areas of responsibility. It is not atypical for several people in an organization to be doing the same job differently. In the press of daily business, they do not share best practices with each other, and the result is inconsistency in delivery and inefficiency in execution of their services. Documenting processes forces employees to team together to establish and then to describe how the tasks are best accomplished. This act of description encourages consensus building and common understanding and appreciation. In addition, the resulting documents help management understand the steps, resources, and effort needed to execute particular steps in a process. Good documentation then becomes a way to articulate expectations and requirements. For some folks, documentation further provides a security blanket that increases their comfort zone because they know what is expected of them and can use the documents to help them do their work.

All documents used by the service company must be reviewed and approved "for adequacy" before they are released to be used by service employees. Adequacy means the documents describe accurately how the work is done. Registrar auditors typically expect to see that the senior individual responsible for a particular operation or area/function has reviewed and approved the document. The reviewing authority should be knowledgeable about the process and ensure that the document accurately describes how the work is actually done. As part of the review process, the reviewer is not only verifying the accuracy of the document, but also is implying that the methods it describes are the best practices available for the particular activity/function to accomplish its goals and objectives. There is no requirement in the standard to have reviewers sign copies of the various documents, but one practical way to demonstrate that the document has been reviewed is to have at least one record copy with the appropriate signatures.

Organizations with highly structured processes have a relatively easier time satisfying the requirements of this section of the standard. Manufacturing organizations have operating manuals and various forms and work instructions to guide employees through the routine steps necessary to set up and control machines and to construct or assemble a product. Similarly, back-room service operations with a great deal of structure, such as bank check clearing or insurance claims processing functions, can usually easily flowchart steps in the various tasks employees perform and thus have an easy time documenting their processes.

However, where interactions between employees and customers are the heart of the service transaction, the process of writing procedures to cover these interactions can be daunting. Certainly, with a great many variables in play, it is impossible to think of and describe every possible variation. It is not at all impossible, however, to establish documented procedures to cover these interactions. ISO does not expect you to document every potential situation or eventuality. The point is to think through the purpose of the transaction and identify approaches, and heuristics, and general rules-of-thumb employees can use.

In many ways, it is more valuable to have documented procedures to support service providers who interact with customers than for manufacturing processes. This is particularly true when a service employee must respond promptly and effectively to a customer requirement, such as when there has been a breakdown in the promised service. For example, hotel clerks or airline reservation clerks need to know how to recover when a reservation is lost or incorrect. Similarly, ambulance emergency medical technicians must know how to respond in a life-threatening crisis. Work guides can help employees recover in these types of situations by laying out some general ground rules to help them decide what to do.

There are at least two possible strategies/solutions for developing documentation for such service groups. The first is to write general steps and focus on outcomes for the service. These types of procedures should focus on how to think through commonly occurring situations and give some specific help in resolution. An *if-then chart,* for example, is an excellent two-column format for such documentation. It lists several possible situations in one column and provides the appropriate action for the employee in the second column. Similarly, a *decision tree chart* will help employees learn to diagnose various situations and select appropriate responses. Case studies and group discussion as part of training programs can help employees learn to think their way through various situations and give them confidence that they will be able to respond appropriately in various situations. Having reference documents after such training strengthens employee responses and moves the company toward meeting this ISO requirement.

Another strategy is to establish measurable parameters within which service employees can operate and in which they can understand what is expected of them. These parameters provide guidance within which employees are empowered to act and establish limits beyond which they are required to seek assistance or approval. For example, a scheduling clerk may be empowered to authorize two hours of overtime for a service technician if it appears a job is running long or if there is a pressing need to satisfy a customer. However, an emergency medical technician may be required to obtain a doctor's approval before administering a certain treatment in the field.

Documentation must be available to every employee who needs it. This means employees need ready access to the documents they actually use, not that every employee must have a copy of every document. Employees also must have access to a master list of current documents and their revisions so they can be sure they are working with the most recent version or revision of the document. Again, not every employee needs the master list, but they do need reasonable access to it.

You must have a proactive program to gather and eliminate all obsolete and out-of-date documents. If some individuals want to keep prior revisions of documents for some reason—perhaps for historical or legal reasons—these must be appropriately marked so no one inadvertently uses them, thinking they represent the current revision.

An important element in this section is your definition of the term *current*. There may be several current revisions of a document in use. For example, a set of operating or maintenance instructions for a machine may be current, even though a newer machine and its maintenance instructions are also in use. It is necessary to maintain the older set of documents for the older machine.

All documents and changes to documents must be reviewed and approved by knowledgeable or responsible individuals. And the reviewer must be provided with information explaining why a document was changed. That does not mean a lengthy written report or explanation needs to be provided. The information may be given to the reviewers verbally, although a note or short memo may be more appropriate in some organizations.

PRACTICAL EXAMPLES

- To ensure the *"pertinent issues of appropriate documents are available at all locations"* where needed, an information technology computer group in a warehouse operation may list and control changes to all of the computer screens data-entry clerks use. Note: computer screens through which work is accomplished count as forms and therefore are considered documents for ISO purposes.
- To ensure documents are *"reviewed and approved for adequacy by authorized personnel prior to issue,"* the attorneys at a life insurance company may review and approve the standard form and wording of clauses within life insurance policies the company sells.
- To ensure documents are *"readily available,"* a university faculty member may put selected journal articles and books on reserve in the university library for members of the class.

COMPLYING WITH SECTION 4.5 IN SERVICE ORGANIZATIONS

Avoid the Temptation to Generalize

Some new ISO practitioners make the mistake of thinking that if they do not write very much or if they write very generalized procedures, the registrar auditors will not be able to write a nonconformance against their processes. Wrong. If your documentation is inadequate for your needs, the auditors will write a major nonconformance against your quality system because you have not adequately described your system. Then you will have flunked your audit and will not be registered. Experienced auditors can determine if you do not have adequate documentation by finding errors or significant variation from the documentation compared to how individuals actually work. They will also carefully question employees to determine how well they know their jobs and if the documentation provided to them is adequate. Your employees are your best measure of what documents they need. You must devise a reasonable solution that works well for your company and employees. You must write sufficiently detailed procedures that are useful while avoiding the opposite error of writing too many and overly detailed procedures. Overwritten or excessive procedures hinder flexibility and bog down processes. There are general rules-of-thumb to help you think about this issue (see Chapter 6, "Quality System"). However, no two organizations can expect to follow the same specific rules. After you satisfy the basic requirements specified in the standard, you must write enough documentation to support your own needs.

Write Short/Concise Procedures

Anyone with a word processor can write a 40-page incomprehensible procedure that no one can use. The real challenge is to write short, concise, and useful procedures. But there are some efficient and practical approaches. Many practitioners have adopted a flowchart documentation strategy to describe the steps in their processes. They also use grammar-checkers to control complexity and write to the sixth-grade reading level, regardless of the level of sophistication or education of their employees. This does not represent condescension; it makes the documents clearer and more likely to be used by everyone.

Involve SMEs and Build Ownership

SMEs—subject matter experts—are the folks who do the work. They know the processes and how best to perform them. If you work with your SMEs as you develop your procedures and work instructions, and if you allow them the freedom to add and contribute to the writing process, the documents are likely to be accurate reflections of the work. Further, the SMEs will take an interest in the accuracy of the documents and gain ownership in them. Some companies elect to train SMEs to write their own procedures. This tactic works, but it is difficult to manage and yields uneven results, especially in the style and level of detail among various writers. A more efficient method is to have a few well-trained document writers work directly with SMEs to develop the procedures and work instructions.

Make the Procedure Change Process-Friendly

Keeping documentation current is a challenge, especially in service organizations with highly fluid and changing settings. A cumbersome or bureaucratic update process will not only annoy your employees, but they will actively avoid the punishment of working with the process. You must make the change and approval process not only painless but also friendly. Employees must be encouraged to actively improve processes and then to willingly update the related documentation. Encouragements need not be elaborate or expensive. Small individual awards, periodic group or team recognition, and, best of all, forms that are easy to complete, and making quick decisions on proposed changes will encourage employees to improve processes and update documentation.

Avoid Differentiating Between Controlled and Uncontrolled Copies

Sometimes companies will try to dodge the challenge of keeping their documents under control by trying to differentiate between controlled and uncontrolled copies—no such distinction should be made. They mistakenly believe they can maintain a few controlled copies while allowing employees to use copies marked "uncontrolled" in their work. They then give employees the responsibility of making sure they have the correct revision of the document. This approach is unrealistic because it is easy for a registrar auditor to find someone using an out-of-date, "uncontrolled" copy of a document. The requirements of this section of the standard are very clear, and even though they are challenging to comply with, attempts to create a "magic work-around" inevitably lead to trouble.

Go Paperless

If at all possible, go paperless. Keep all of your documentation—or as much as possible—on-line. Control access to limit changes. Provide terminals or access for individuals who need to have access. The hardware requirements and learning curve may be expensive, but the benefits soon pay for the expense.

CASE STUDY IN DOCUMENT AND DATA CONTROL

Lawton-Russell, Inc., in Chicago is a 10-person investment advisory company. Their primary financial service is managing profit-sharing plans and retirement plans for small and medium-sized business owners who have qualified plans but need superior investment management services. They succeed against their much larger competitors, despite fees that are competitive or slightly higher than the market, because they focus on offering a premium service to customers for whom such service is the compelling reason to select an investment advisor.

President Gregory Lawton started on the road to ISO registration after he heard a presentation on the Malcolm Baldrige National Quality Award (MBNQA) given by the CEO of the Ritz-Carlton Hotel Chain. Like the Ritz staff, Gregory and his staff are obsessed with good service as a way to attract and keep clients and to differentiate themselves from their competition, and Lawton saw value in applying for the MBNQA. Rather than immediately targeting a Baldrige application, however, Gregory chose ISO registration as a first-step strategic business investment. He saw ISO as a way to formalize the company's quality structures and provide third-party verification—similar to an accounting audit verification—of their quality systems. He also recognized that registration would demonstrate Lawton-Russell's service levels to their current clients and serve as a powerful selection criterion for new clients.

Since the level of education and professionalism among the staff was very high, the challenge was not to manage the actual procedure writing process. All members of the company are capable communicators; excellent communication skills serve as a foundation of their success with clients. Instead, in large measure because their service is so personal and based on establishing one-on-one relationships with their clients, the challenge was to find ways to adequately describe processes without overgeneralizing or making the procedures overly detailed or confining.

It took the staff about four months to complete and test their procedures and work instructions. The staff found that they did not need to fundamentally change any of their processes because these were serving staff and their clients well. However, during the testing stage, where they checked to see if the written procedures adequately reflected their actual performance, they were able to share insights and seek best practices among the group, and thus improve the quality of their service. It took some time to create the documented foundation, but the time invested had an extra dividend because they were able to incorporate the work instructions into a computer-based system that made them instantly available as needed.

The most important outcome from their documentation system, however, has been the positive response they received from everyone in the office. At first, several individuals thought ISO documentation was going to be burdensome. In fact, it turned out to be a great support to operations because everyone in the organization now knows the responsibilities of each member and can share ways to coordinate activities and improve individual performances. The documentation also serves to support personal performance reviews; individual members can assess their performances against the desired best practices and outcomes. Finally, an established program rewards members when they find ways to improve processes and update procedures in support of the company's goal of providing the best possible financial investment advice and service to business owners.

LESSONS LEARNED

It is an unhappy fact of ISO life that most nonconformances written by internal auditors and registrar auditors are written against documentation failures or inconsistencies. There are several reasons for this. First, a great many people think procedures and paperwork are a major pain and, therefore, seek to avoid doing it thoughtfully or it at all. Second, there is a myth that documentation slows service. Certainly, service persons often are rushed, and, when face-to-face with a customer, are not likely to want to stop to consult a procedure before responding to the customer's needs. But having documentation does not mean that it must be referred to in each service instance. It should serve as a reference and guide, especially for nonroutine situations. A well-trained employee should not need to refer regularly to procedures.

Despite these apparent negatives, however, good documentation serves companies powerfully in several ways. First, the act of writing and developing documentation forces management to articulate its expectations and for employees to share best practices. This process alone is worth the energy and thought invested. Many companies have found that through the examination of their processes for documentation, they can improve the processes and get the benefits of efficiency, waste reduction, and cost control. Second, good documentation supports consistency in the services provided. This is another extraordinarily positive outcome for the investment in documentation. Third, good documentation is an excellent training tool to help new service persons learn their jobs. A final unanticipated outcome is that many companies find the process of writing ISO documents is an excellent housecleaning exercise that forces folks to get rid of all the accumulated and outdated memos, notes, and "corporate wisdom" that has grown moldy in the bottoms of various desk drawers.

10

~✦ ✦~

Section 4.6, Purchasing

Section 4.6, Purchasing, asks:

1. Do our vendors understand our needs?
2. Are our vendors able to provide the products and services that we need?

INTERPRETING THE STANDARD

This section of the standard is very similar to Section 4.3, Contract Review. Whereas Contract Review requires you to define your relationship with your customers, this section of the standard requires you to define your relationship with your vendors and subcontractors. The section first requires a procedure to describe how your company buys products and services from vendors and subcontractors. Along with maintaining a record of acceptable subcontractors, this section of the standard requires your service company to have:

- A process to ensure your company buys goods and services from vendors that can meet your needs
- A way to evaluate vendors to make sure they are able to satisfy your company's needs, including evaluating the vendor's quality assurance program
- A clearly established definition of how much and what type of control your service company will exercise over its vendors

- Purchase orders and ordering documents that clearly describe the product ordered, including data, models, numbers, or other specific descriptors
- A review and approval process to ensure that purchasing documents are correct and satisfy your service company's needs before they are released to the vendor

There are some additional requirements if you decide to conduct inspections and evaluations at the vendor's location before the vendor ships or delivers the product or service to you. These include clearly defining the way the product or service is inspected and released at the vendor's location; and making sure that, when it is so specified in the contract, a customer of yours has access to inspect the product or service at your vendor's location.

In some settings, the service company's customer also may require you to use a particular subcontractor for the goods or services you provide. Even though your customer requires you to use a particular vendor, in these cases you remain responsible for making sure your vendor delivers a satisfactory product or service to you. The fact that your customer requires you to use a vendor does not relieve your company from responsibility or subsequent rejection of the product or service by your customer. In short, even though you have followed your customer's orders to use a particular vendor, the customer may still reject your service. ISO does not allow anyone to pass the buck!

There is one additional very interesting idea in this section of the standard. As part of the process of qualifying vendors, the standard suggests service companies consider potential vendors' quality assurance programs as one selection criterion. Obviously, any ISO-registered company that must qualify its vendors will ask potential vendors if they are ISO-registered. Thus, the ISO standard has a built-in motivator to promote the adoption and use of the ISO standard.

SERVICE PERSPECTIVES ON PURCHASING

This section of the standard mirrors the requirements found in Section 4.3, Contract Review, this time defining your relationship with your vendors, rather than your relationship with your customers, as specified in Contract Review. In both cases, the basic questions are: "Do we understand what the other party wants?" and "Are we able to provide the service our customer wants/Is the vendor able to provide the product or service we want?"

Many medium and large service companies have fairly sophisticated purchasing processes in place. These may focus largely on volume/price considerations to meet the organization's financial needs. Smaller companies may be doing "hip-pocket" purchasing successfully, in an informal and relationship-based way. That is, the one or two individuals in charge know what they are doing and from whom they are buying. They may have all information neatly stored in their heads. Neither approach is necessarily adequate to satisfy the ISO requirements.

When thinking about applying this section of the standard, the key words are "ensure that purchased product . . . conforms to specified requirements." Remember, ISO defines "product" as both products and services. *Specified requirements* are generated from a variety of sources. In addition to requirements to satisfy the customer, all internal customers must have their needs met as well. Essentially, this section of the standard requires purchasing persons to adopt a broad world-view and satisfy needs of internal and external customers, in addition to attending to their typical charter of price management.

PRACTICAL EXAMPLES

- To *"evaluate and select subcontractors,"* a hotel manager may visit a uniform laundry service to assess the service's ability to provide clean sheets, table linens, and uniforms.
- To ensure *"documents shall contain data clearly describing the product ordered,"* a purchasing manager may compare solicited bids from competing long-distance telephone companies and select a provider based on service and billing arrangements.
- To *"verify purchased product at the subcontractor's premises,"* an independent association of grocery store owners may assess the quality of meat butchering by conducting a quality practices review at the butcher's location.

COMPLYING WITH SECTION 4.6 IN SERVICE ORGANIZATIONS

Define Purchased Product

Begin by identifying all of the products and services that are purchased. Establish three or four categories of purchased products/services and describe the methods used to select vendors in each category. Avoid the pitfall of naming categories in qualitative terms. Terms such as *important, critical,* or *quality* may lead to philosophical discussions about the definition of the category rather than on the important issue of how the process is supposed to work. Nonevaluative terms such as *repair, administrative, disposable,* and the like define how the product/service is used, making it much easier to assign purchased items to such categories. Once categories are established, it's possible to describe for each category how vendors are qualified and how products and services are purchased.

Identify all Vendors

There is no requirement in the standard to have a master list of all vendors, but such a list frequently will help you make sure you limit your purchases to qualified vendors. A database is a convenient way to maintain such a list. A marked-up copy of the local yellow pages is an unsatisfactory tactic to meet this requirement because you must evaluate vendors. The yellow pages publishers usually include a disclaimer that states that, although someone advertises in the yellow pages, it does not necessarily mean the publisher has verified them as competent or capable to deliver the products or services advertised.

Qualify Vendors

The standard does not require vendors to be "certified," which implies a fairly complex and rigorous undertaking with rules and requirements established by a certifying agency, such as a government regulatory entity or industry/professional organization. The standard instead requires your company to define how you qualify vendors. Useful tools for qualification both before and during delivery of products and services include past experience with a vendor, contract review processes, incoming inspections, in-process assessments, and follow-up evaluations. In fact, you may *grandperson* vendors with whom you have had a successful relationship and good experience.

Not all vendors must be qualified according to the same criteria. A system of three or four product/service categories will allow you to apply more rigorous demands to certain vendors, while limiting the amount of attention required for routine types of purchases.

Revisit Purchasing Documents and Forms

The standard requires there be adequate descriptions of the product or service being purchased, containing sufficient information and detail about the purchased item so both buyer and seller know what to expect. Purchasing documents and the data they contain must be reviewed for adequacy before they are released.

Evaluate the usefulness of data you require on purchasing documents and forms and question their formats. Frequently, these forms can be simplified. It is possible the forms themselves are well-designed and useful for purchasing personnel. However, internal customers may not have an easy time understanding what information is required or how to fill out the forms.

Establish Communication Links

Although the connections are not immediately obvious, this section of the standard links to several other sections of the standard. Communications between all parties involved in identifying purchase needs and negotiating the purchases must flow smoothly in order to successfully meet the purchasing requirements. There is an obvious connection between Purchasing and Contract Review (Section 4.3). Other connect points include Design Review (Section 4.4.6), where purchasing personnel have a role to play to ensure that purchased services and products will support the design. Also, there may be a direct link to Corrective and Preventive Action (Section 4.14), as a self-evaluation device to ensure that both internal and external customers are satisfied with the products and services bought through the purchasing process.

Consider ISO Registration to Qualify Vendors

The standard allows—and encourages—you to qualify vendors based on their quality assurance processes. One of the easiest ways to do this is to ask potential suppliers if they are ISO-registered. Some companies that have stringent qualification vendor requirements—because of the nature of their business or because there is a statutory requirement to do so—have used this technique to shift the cost of conducting site visits and qualifying vendors from their own budget to the vendor's. That is, the potential vendor bears the cost of achieving ISO registration, and the customer does not have to use resources to conduct audits or qualification processes. In fact, in some cases, a copy of the vendor's ISO registration certificate is all some customers require to qualify the vendor.

CASE STUDY IN PURCHASING

The approach of the medical practice of Dr. Mark Figgie and Dr. Richard Laskin exemplifies how service organizations can manage and benefit from the requirements of Section 4.6, Purchasing. The orthopedic surgery practice of Drs. Figgie and Laskin in New York City focuses primarily on serving arthritis patients. In addition to the two physicians, six medical and administrative persons work in the offices, including Jack Davis, their nurse clinician and ISO 9000 Management Representative. The doctors' offices are co-located with the 140-bed Hospital for Special Surgery (HSS) where about 50 surgeons practice.

The doctors knew they were providing quality care to their patients. But given the radical changes underway in the health care industry, including cost containment and insurance reimbursement issues, as nurse clinician Jack Davis related, they decided they wanted a mechanism that would help them demonstrate the level of quality that they had achieved. They saw ISO registration as one way to do this.

They started by refining the documentation in their already existing medical protocols. These protocols satisfied most of the ISO 9001 requirements. However, as they were going through the documentation process, they recognized opportunities to improve how they performed many of their activities. They focused initially on improving their processes rather than on trying to think about applying the ISO standard. The changes they made in their activities, therefore, were done not to satisfy the requirements of the ISO standard, but rather as a result of looking at their own methods and finding ways to improve them. These resulted in a better organized and smoother flow to their daily office and medical practice activities.

For example, Davis said, rather than taking a medical history during the patient's first visit, they now send the medical history form to the patient in advance to fill out at home before the patient's first office visit. This simple change provides patients plenty of time to find all the necessary information and be able to give the doctors a complete medical history. It is particularly important to make sure the patient reports all medications currently being taken so the doctors can be alerted to potential counterindications and conflicts among medications. In addition to being assured that they have complete information, the doctors are now able to spend more time during the first visit interviewing the patient and discussing his or her history, rather than waiting for the patient to struggle to remember information. This simple change now allows the doctors to focus with the patient on his or her current needs rather than focusing on the history-gathering process.

Because much of the doctors' surgery practice and patient care is conducted at the Hospital for Special Surgery, it is absolutely critical the doctors and the hospital have a close relationship. The doctors consider the hospital a subcontractor to their practice, and they used Section 4.6, Purchasing, to establish a memorandum of understanding with the hospital to define this relationship. The hospital provides both products and services to the practice. Products include routine office medical supplies and equipment. Services include pre- and post-surgery patient medical care. Obviously, both—and in particular the latter—would greatly affect the doctors' patients and the quality of care the doctors are able to provide to their patients.

The memorandum of understanding between the doctors and the hospital covers daily administrative support as well as patient medical support. Particularly useful is the framework for communication established by the memorandum, especially when difficulties arise, when misunderstandings occur, or when someone discovers an opportunity for improvement. The issues could be related to patient care, administrative routines, or clinical practices. The issue might be related to any number of causes—training, communication, misunderstandings, or questions in administrative practices. Regardless, they use their purchasing memorandum of understanding and their corrective and preventive action program to allow them to sit down together and work through the issues in a mutually supporting and structured problem-solving manner rather than in a confrontational or accusatory way. ISO has provided the doctors and their hospital a framework within which to define and effectively maintain their working relationship with each other.

LESSONS LEARNED

Drs. Figgie's and Laskin's experience with ISO demonstrates many of the advantages of seeking registration, and they did many things right along the way to achieving that goal. First, they started from a firm basis with a good quality foundation. They were able to rationalize seeking registration as a way to help themselves and their practice, rather than simply gaining a certificate to hang on the wall. They are using their ISO program in their daily administrative and medical practices to help them improve their protocols. At the same time, registration provides them with a way to demonstrate the quality of their practice. For example, it has helped them demonstrate compliance to the FDA and avoid redundancies by relying on their memorandum of understanding with the Hospital for Special Surgery to conduct many of their purchasing activities.

In addition, the doctors have recognized the interconnected links inherent in the ISO standard. On its surface, the purchasing requirements would seem to be focused on the mechanics of purchasing activities. However, in order to effectively administer a purchasing program, good communication with both internal and external customers must exist. And there must be a willingness on the part of all parties to work together to make sure that "purchased product . . . conforms to specified requirements."

11

~ৰ ৮~

Section 4.7, Control of Customer-Supplied Product

THE KEY QUESTION

Section 4.7, Control of Customer-Supplied Product, asks:

1. Are we protecting things—such as products, services, or information—that our customer gives to us and we use in the service we provide back to our customer?

INTERPRETING THE STANDARD

Customer-Supplied Product (CSP) refers to any product or service provided to your company by your customers that you use to provide your finished service to them. On its surface, this arrangement may seem foreign to service companies. It is a frequent arrangement in many manufacturing settings, however. It is more prevalent in service organizations than may be evident initially, particularly when information is considered as a customer-supplied product. On a personal level, we provide information about our financial condition when we apply for loans, we provide information about our health histories when we visit a new medical provider, and we divulge address, telephone number, and credit-card information with a wide variety of transactions. Virtually every service organization may find ways to apply this section of the standard.

In addition to a workable procedure for handling, storing, and integrating information provided by customers, a good process for managing and documenting customer interactions results in quick resolution to CSP concerns and issues. This section of the standard stipulates two *shalls* and requires one record. They are:

- A procedure that controls verification, storage, and maintenance of customer-supplied product. Essentially, the procedure must describe how you deal with this requirement
- A procedure showing how lost, damaged, or unsuitable product or service is recorded and reported to the customer. ISO wants you to communicate with your customer and resolve inadequacies or problems. It is inappropriate to disregard a problem simply because it is the customer's fault
- A record of the report made to the customer. The record provides objective evidence you have communicated with the customer and resolved the problem(s)

SERVICE PERSPECTIVES ON CUSTOMER-SUPPLIED PRODUCT

Of the 20 sections in the ISO 9001 standard, Customer-Supplied Product, on its surface, may appear to be the least applicable to service organizations. However, many service organizations will find applications of the requirements relevant to their needs. In traditional manufacturing situations, this section is applied in situations where one company receives a product, part, or component from its customer and incorporates that item into its own product, which the company then sells back in finished form to its customer. Consider a food producer that packs house brands. The packer receives packaging materials from its customer, packs the product in the customer's packaging, and sells the finished and packaged goods back to the customer. Another example is when a component manufacturer requires suppliers to use subcomponents from its own product line in assembling goods it buys from them. For example, a computer chip manufacturer may require a computer manufacturer to use its chips in the computers it sells to the chip maker.

Customer-Supplied Product in service organizations usually focuses on customer-supplied information. For example, a bank or hospital must use the information provided by customers to develop or arrange service for the customers. The bank uses customer information to extend credit or provide banking services. Hospitals and doctors use customer-supplied information to determine treatments and insurance eligibility. These two examples satisfy the concept of Customer-Supplied Product because the supplier uses and incorporates the information into their service. It is also possible for a customer to supply your company with a service, in which case this would be considered customer-supplied service. In situations where customer-supplied information is the primary concern, the company usually must establish some framework to protect confidentiality and assure the accuracy of the customer's information.

A key to this definition is that the service organization must transform the customer-supplied product or service. Money a bank customer deposits is not a customer-supplied product because the bank does not transform the money in some way before returning it to the depositor. Similarly, luggage transported by an airline is not a customer-supplied product. The luggage is transported, not transformed, by the airline.

Customer-supplied service may include an arrangement where the customer has their employees working at your service company to facilitate an activity. For example, your customer may be a software developer who provides you with training and technical support for your computer network. You in turn use this network as part of the service that you deliver to the software developer. Whether the exchange is customer-supplied product or customer-supplied service, the same requirements apply. Remember, ISO sees service activities as part of its definition of the term *product*.

PRACTICAL EXAMPLES

- To establish *"procedures for the control,"* a bank's loan department would initiate confidentiality policies for the use of customer-supplied information to make a decision to provide financing to a customer for a new home loan. They also have a process to verify the accuracy of the information provided by the customer.
- To ensure *"verification"* of customer-supplied product, a health insurance company would cross-check individual policy coverage against information from their medical providers—doc-

tors and hospitals—in order to determine and approve payment of medical claims.

- To respond when *"such product that is lost, damaged, or is otherwise unsuitable for use,"* a transhipment consolidator may inspect customer-supplied packaging as part of their arrangement to package, consolidate, and provide overseas shipment of the customer's products.

COMPLYING WITH SECTION 4.7 IN SERVICE ORGANIZATIONS

Distinguish CSP and Purchasing

Sometimes a customer will require you, by contract, to use the service or product of a particular subcontractor who has been approved by your customer. Do not misinterpret this situation as customer-supplied product. Such arrangements are better handled as part of Section 4.6, Purchasing.

Evaluate Whether CSP Applies to You

In most service organizations, it may be more efficient to handle CSP situations within other elements of the standard and thereby eliminate the need to address this section at all. If you do not deal with Customer-Supplied Product, you should write two short sentences in your quality manual. The first sentence should state that this section of the standard is not relevant to your operation or you effectively handle these matters under other elements of the standard. The second sentence should state that if such a relationship with a customer were to become part of your quality system, you will establish, maintain, and document a procedure that meets the ISO 9001 standard requirements.

Accept Responsibility for Problems

Interestingly enough, the standard makes the statement that your customer is responsible for providing you with acceptable product/service. However, if your customer is not an ISO-registered company, this requirement has no force. In any case, this section effectively prevents you from finger-pointing at your customer. It is specifically designed to forestall a loophole that would allow you to excuse yourself from responsibility for a problem. Essentially, ISO says you must identify and own the problem through to its resolution. You must resolve the issue to adhere to the requirements of Section 1.0, Scope, to satisfy your customer. The requirement for a report will help protect you and demonstrate compliance during an ISO audit. Usually, a report could be a form or a memo to file indicating the customer was contacted, a short description of the problem, and a brief explanation of how it was resolved.

Link CSP to Your Sales Processes

Sales and marketing personnel who typically handle contract review—and whose commissions are affected by their ability to consummate the sale—may be less motivated to deal with what they perceive as mundane details that may delay their order. The groups who must deliver on the contract, however, see these issues as crucial to their success and prefer to have this issue controlled under their procedure for customer-supplied product. Make sure that you have buy-in from your sales forces and that you share mutually supporting efforts to serve the customer and satisfy the ISO standard requirements.

CASE STUDY IN CUSTOMER-SUPPLIED PRODUCT

BC TEL Education, the training division of BC TELECOM, Inc. in Canada, is an interesting case study for several reasons. First, their ISO registration is for a 140-person training division, rather than the entire company. This division, separate from but supported by their corporate organization, sought and obtained ISO registration. They are not an independent entity, yet their registration applies only to the training function.

Second, according to Arch McFarlan, who led their ISO registration process, no external driver motivated the training group to seek registration. BC TELECOM, located in Burnaby, near Vancouver, provides local, long-distance, and mobile telephone service, as well as a range of other communication services to the province of British Columbia, much like the Baby Bells in the United States. The training division took the lead to become registered in order to investigate ways that might help them improve their service to their customers—the rest of the company. The training division also served as a test case to determine the value of ISO registration and also to be a resource to other divisions of BC TELECOM that might be seeking registration.

Customer-Supplied Product is an infrequent but important concern for BC TEL Education. In addition to providing training on a range of soft topics, such as time management, marketing and sales, and customer service, the division provides skill-based training for technicians and operations personnel. Further, in addition to providing skills-based training to their own employees, they also provide similar training to other telephone companies both in Canada and the United States. For example, they provide technician training on central office telephone switches. Essentially, a telephone switch is hardware and software that ensures a call is routed to the right subscriber's telephone. When BC TEL Education conducts hands-on switch training for external customers, they often use the customer's switch at the customer's location. It is vital that the hardware and software requirements for the switch are clearly communicated between the customer and BC TEL Education so the trainees and instructors are working with the correct release of hardware and software, and that they are fully functional.

The BC TEL Education procedure for dealing with questions of Customer-Supplied Product is closely linked with its contract review procedure. It clearly establishes responsibilities and authorities to ensure that the customer's current software revisions and hardware models are available for hands-on training, lesson materials are appropriately keyed to the software and hardware, the instructor is knowledgeable about the specific equipment and software, and the associated learning materials—for example, performance measures, texts, and manuals—are appropriate.

LESSONS LEARNED

When Control of Customer-Supplied Product is an infrequent issue, it usually can be handled as a function within Section 4.3, Contract Review. If so, it might be wise to avoid the need for an additional procedure by dealing with these issues there. If your company elects to use a separate procedure for Control of Customer-Supplied Product, you must carefully determine and articulate who is responsible for what and how internal issues within the company will be resolved. It is particularly important to avoid conflicts between the Contract Review procedure and the procedure for Control of Customer-Supplied Product.

12

⌁ ❧ ❦ ⌁

Section 4.8,
Product Identification
and Traceability

THE KEY QUESTION

Section 4.8, Product Identification and Traceability, asks:

1. If we need to, can we identify our service or the components of our service?

INTERPRETING THE STANDARD

This section of the standard, which deals with identifying and tracking product, is the only one that starts with the words "where appropriate." It specifies that the company shall have a procedure to control this activity. In manufacturing settings, products or batches are frequently assigned an identification number. This might be a serial number on a valve, a VIN (vehicle identification number) on an automobile, or a batch number on a can of tuna or bottle of aspirin.

For manufacturers of products, the rationale of the section is to be able to provide a trail to research problems or concerns that may show up after the product is in the hands of the consumer. For example, auto manufacturers want to be able to notify car buyers if there is a need to recall a particular auto model or production run. Similarly, pharmaceutical, food, or other consumable producer companies need to be able to pull product from the shelves if a problem is discovered. As importantly, the identifiers help company researchers trace back to their own production runs and be able to investigate subassemblies, parts, and materials provided by vendors. The company may be able, for example to pinpoint a cause for a defect or problem on a vendor's product or service. Similarly, a manufacturer may be able to help a customer by being able to identify product. For example, some insulation manufacturers were able to save money for owners of public buildings—particularly schools—during the great asbestos scare because they were able to tell school districts if any asbestos was used in the insulation in each building.

In addition to a procedure, ISO requires the company to maintain identification control throughout the stages of production, delivery, and installation. When required either by the customer, a code or standard, or for any reason your company itself deems wise, you need a system to identify unique items or batches. Finally, methods and records of the identifiers need to be established.

SERVICE PERSPECTIVES ON PRODUCT IDENTIFICATION AND TRACEABILITY

This section of the standard exemplifies the type of difficulty ISO's language and manufacturing bias presents to service providers. Because products are tangible, it is possible to put a number or unique identifier on the item. However, services are frequently intangibles, and it may be tempting to try to excuse or side-step this requirement. Also, because the initial "where appropriate" language seems to offer easy forgiveness, service providers may fail to appreciate the advantages of using the product identification and traceability provisions. Service providers must first determine the value of using this section of the standard.

Product Identification and Traceability are useful ways to protect the company. The service company must decide what risks are possible or likely, and how identification and traceability may provide some measure of protection. It is also possible to use this section of the standard to improve customer service. For example, a computer technical support group might use an incident number system for calls to their service center. At the conclusion of the service call, the technician provides the customer with the incident number and also enters that number into the customer's record against the customer's equipment serial number. The technician makes notes into the data incident database so that if the customer continues to have difficulty, the next technician can see what has been done. If the second technician needs to revisit the same problem, it is possible to study the results and determine the effectiveness of the first call solution. Also, the incidents can be categorized so service management can see trends in similar problems and perhaps post a solution in the company's fax-back or FAQ (Frequently Asked Questions) on-line support services.

PRACTICAL EXAMPLES

- In order to identify *"the product by suitable means,"* a theater/event ticket service may identify an individual's tickets and maintain a database to identify to whom they were shipped. This product identification would allow the provider to settle claims against lost tickets.
- To establish *"unique identification of individual product or batches,"* a recycling waste collection service provider may give its customers containers of different colors to categorize types of product collected.
- To maintain *"traceability,"* a lawn sprinkler installer may maintain a diagram for the customer showing where water lines and sprinkler heads are located in the customer's grounds.

COMPLYING WITH SECTION 4.8 IN SERVICE ORGANIZATIONS

Assess the Risk

An identification program is an insurance policy against future difficulties. It should be driven by realization of some level of concern or potential downside that establishes a need for the information provided through the identification and traceability effort. Because of the cost to run such a program, there must be a reasonable use for it. If the service provider cannot clearly identify a requirement for traceability (the need for which is indicated by the standard's language "where appropriate"), then it is inadvisable to mount the effort.

Collect Useful Data

Useful metrics need to be associated with the identification and traceability efforts. It is inappropriate to collect data for the simple pleasure of generating numbers. The program needs to help the service company provide better service or improve its competitive position. Further, there should be an efficient way to analyze the collected data and communicate the results of analysis to management to initiate action or as part of their decision-making processes. The data should be available to process improvement teams to help them focus on potential areas for improvement.

Keep the Structure/Data/Records Simple

To be useful, the data must be easily retrievable as well as easily manipulated into useful information that will guide future decisions and process improvements. If such a program is relevant to your service organization's needs, start small and simple and then build slowly as the need becomes better defined and the usefulness of the program is demonstrated. An evolving program that is used is far more relevant than a wonderful database full of unused numbers.

CASE STUDY IN PRODUCT IDENTIFICATION AND TRACEABILITY

Applied Consumer and Clinical Evaluations, Inc., located in Mississauga, Ontario, Canada, provides quantitative and qualitative research on shopper attitudes and desires for consumer package goods. These goods include cleaning products, textiles, health and beauty products, pharmaceuticals, cosmetics, and foods. They use blind and branded tests with consumers to help companies establish brand equity, the value of the brand name that will prompt a consumer to select and purchase one specific brand product over another. Obviously, to be successful, consumer companies want to know which features and aspects of their products particularly appeal to their customers and how to focus on those aspects. They also research customer response to features that help influence buying decisions, such as smell, taste, and texture.

Applied Consumer and Clinical Evaluations, which has 20 full-time and about 50 part-time employees, recruits individuals to serve as test subjects for their research programs. Joan Berta is the Director of Sales and Marketing and their ISO 9000 Management Representative. Working together, members of the company will design and run a research project for a consumer company on a particular product. Although every research project is tailor-made for each product, some general steps—particularly as related to the ISO standard requirements—are common to all research projects. First they design a questionnaire or ballot for each project to generate responses from the participating consumers. These questionnaires include both scoring or rating scales and open-ended questions that require written responses and opinions. For the latter, the company runs a content analysis of the responses to discover similarities and is able to summarize the findings into data useful to the customer. This allows them to look at the data through a variety of prisms and find leads and insight into customer perceptions.

Applied Consumer and Clinical Evaluations uses the product identification and traceability requirements of the ISO standard to identify and track three distinct elements in their process: the consumer, the ballot, and the product. Each has a unique identifier. This is significant because all their tests are blind, that is, individual results are anonymous. A consumer will receive a copy of the questionnaire and either the product being tested or a competing product; he or she is asked to rate or score the product on the ballot provided. Some projects are run at the company's headquarters, and sometimes consumers are given products and log books to use at home. When completed, the ballot is returned to a company employee who performs a quality check to make sure all the ballots have been returned and the information on them has been clearly and fully completed. Frequently, one consumer is asked to respond to questionnaires about several products during a single research session, so it is necessary to make sure all ballots are completed and returned. The identities of the test consumers are hidden from the manufacturer; therefore, it is necessary to have a tracking system for them. Once each consumer has completed and returned all questionnaires, he or she receives an honorarium in return for time and service.

All ballots are quantified and data are evaluated through a variety of statistical techniques to find many ways to look at the data and discern information that will help the customer company make decisions about their products. Usually, all of the raw data and records are maintained for at least six months after the completion of a project. Because these projects generate so much data, and because Applied Consumer and Clinical Evaluations must maintain blind product tests and protect the anonymity of the individual respondents, they rely on Section 4.8, Product Identification and Traceability, to provide clear lines of connection between results and the raw data generated. This section also helps them make sure they have accurately captured and entered all of the data into their statistical database.

LESSONS LEARNED

Like many other service companies, Applied Consumer and Clinical Evaluations did not see dramatic results from their ISO registration project. That is because they had good processes in place before the registration project began. Also like many service companies, they struggled with the terminology and concepts in the standard and how to apply these both in a service setting in general and to their particular needs. As they evaluate their experience now, however, they report that ISO registration has proven especially valuable on several fronts. Registration has helped build overall staff confidence, and it has especially built confidence in their ability to identify and track research subjects, ballots, and products. It has given them a well-structured methodology to maintain control over the diverse elements used in research projects. They are particularly confident now that they can respond appropriately and in detail to questions about their research projects because they have identified the elements in their projects— consumers, products, and ballots—and can efficiently tie them to reported results.

13

~❧ ❧~

Section 4.9,
Process Control

THE KEY QUESTIONS

Section 4.9, Process Control, asks:

1. Do we know what we are doing and how work gets accomplished?
2. Are we consistently providing excellent service to our customers through our ability to control our own internal work processes?

INTERPRETING THE STANDARD

This section of the standard is central to all types of organizations, both manufacturing and service. It asks the company to address, describe, and control all routine work flows, tasks, and activities. The basic requirement is to establish *controlled conditions* within which work is accomplished. A fundamental tenet of control is documentation. A simple definition of controlled conditions is that individuals know what they are supposed to be doing to accomplish their tasks and have the resources to do their work. Essentially, the standard requires the company to establish and describe a framework within which work is accomplished. In addition to a procedure, this section requires that:

- Suitable equipment and working environment are available
- Everyone complies with relevant codes and standards, plans, and procedures

- Process parameters and product characteristics are monitored
- Criteria for workmanship—acceptance criteria—are established
- Equipment is maintained (preventive maintenance)

There is an additional requirement in this section for controlling special processes. In manufacturing settings, a *special process* is an activity that changes a product or component in such a way that it cannot be inspected or changed after the event. For example, welding, painting, and mixing chemicals are all examples of special processes. In these cases, the process either must be continuously monitored or carried out by an experienced operator. Companies that have special processes must maintain records for the processes, related equipment, and personnel.

SERVICE PERSPECTIVES ON PROCESS CONTROL

Of the 20 sections, Process Control is probably the easiest for manufacturing organizations and one of the more difficult for service organizations. As in the requirements for document control, manufacturers have tangible evidence of the steps involved in assembling a product. Similarly, back-room service functions frequently can be highly structured and controlled. However, in one-on-one interpersonal communication situations between service personnel and customers, the range of variables that can effect the transaction is so large it is not possible to identify all of the potential permutations, much less plan for and control each of them.

As in controlling documents, the best approach to establishing process control is to give service personnel the tools they need to help them think their way through various situations and help them understand the limits or parameters of their authority. In effect, one-to-one interactions may be viewed as *special processes* under the ISO definition. As such, they must either be continuously monitored—clearly impractical in most situations—or performed by qualified individuals. Service personnel can become qualified through experience and training. The company can also provide good documentation to support and establish what is expected and what are the limits of the individuals' behaviors and responsibilities.

Striking the right balance in process control and control of documents may be difficult for service organizations. In response to the fundamentally foreign structured approach of ISO and its notion of control, service practitioners frequently overdocument or end by having too little document and/or process control. There is no single right amount of documentation. Despite its seemingly rigid structure, the ISO standard is not a science, and it certainly is not prescriptive. The process of internal auditing is really an art form of assessing what is needed for a particular company. In the end, the process is probably in control and the documentation is probably adequate if:

- Service personnel are comfortable with their jobs
- They know what they are doing
- The process is delivering the service fairly consistently
- The company is not in a constant fire-fighting mode
- There are few needs for corrections or apologies to customers because of errors, delays and failures

Practical Examples

- To ensure that *"processes are carried out under controlled conditions,"* an airline may require pilots to circulate the aircraft cabin air every two hours.
- To overcome the situation that *"results of processes cannot be fully verified by subsequent inspection and testing,"* a house painting company may decide to hire only painters with three years of demonstrated experience.
- To monitor and control *"suitable process parameters and product characteristics,"* supervisors in a computer technical support service center periodically may listen to service calls between customers and service technicians.

Complying With Section 4.9 in Service Organizations

Understand How Work Is Accomplished

Creative geniuses among us do not routinely seek registration to ISO 9000. However, most employees are not creative geniuses able to improvise novel solutions at every turn. Nor do most service organizations want extreme creativity (advertising and public relations agencies notwithstanding). Instead, they want reliable and consistent responses to customer needs. Organizations build and support structured tasks and activities. Regardless of the pace of change or the degree of flexibility and empowerment within an organization, fundamental critical processes continue to be established and followed. ISO requires your service company to define and describe these primary processes. You must understand their steps, tasks, activities, and outcomes—that is, how your organization goes about accomplishing its objectives.

Define Authorities and Responsibilities

The subclauses within this section of the standard have a strong flavor of the manufacturing perspective of the standard writers. In spite of this, the applicability to service organizations is clear. You must know who has responsibilities and authorities to ensure that the work is accomplished correctly. An examination of subclauses *a* through *g*, for example, really boils down to understanding who does what and who is responsible for what. The applicability to service companies is especially clear in Section 4.1.2.1, where the standard stipulates that authorities and responsibilities shall be defined "particularly for personnel who need the organizational freedom" to prevent and/or correct errors. For service organizations, the seven subclauses in Section 4.9, which articulate the kinds of activities over which you must assign individuals responsibility, serve as suggestions only. You must determine what are the primary activities in your company—the primary processes—and ensure that duties and responsibilities are established to control them. This is Process Control.

Control Does Not Equal Inflexibility

An often heard, but inaccurate, complaint against ISO registration in general and Section, 4.9, Process Control, in particular is that they inhibit flexibility, creativity, and change. Rigid work processes that prevent rapid response to changing customer needs are entirely contrary to the fundamental underlying philosophy of ISO. The importance of that philosophy is clearly stated in Section 1, the Scope statement, which requires you to satisfy your customers. If your ISO program impedes your ability to serve your customers, you have failed to understand the basics of ISO or have failed to initiate a system that meets the requirements of the standard. In effect, you have wasted your time.

CASE STUDY IN PROCESS CONTROL

Health Risk Management, Inc. (HRM) processes medical and dental claims and provides other back-office operations for several employee and health care organizations. They have 750 employees in Minneapolis and 150 employees in Kalamazoo, as well as branch operations in other cities in the United States and Canada. HRM had tracked the ISO movement for several years, but was initially put off by the standard's manufacturing orientation and language. However, their CEO decided to pursue registration as a way to demonstrate the quality of their operations. They reasoned that registration was a way to position the company in the high-level competition and cost-consciousness of the health care industry today.

According to Thomas Spitznagle, Vice President, Strategic Planning, in Minneapolis, the need to establish process control procedures came at an opportune moment for the company. Work on revamping their computer-based systems highlighted a known difficulty: none of the offices were using the same processes to handle claims. Developing their ISO processes gave them the chance to adopt common methods to complete their work while at the same time it provided an opportunity to enhance their computer-based systems.

According to Gary Fergemann, their ISO Management Representative in Kalamazoo, the claims management business is particularly complex because each customer company's benefit plan may contain different levels of insurance coverage. Further, different groups within a company may have different kinds of benefits. Therefore, careful controls on how claims are paid against the specifications of the company's contract are vitally important. According to Tom and Gary, as a first step to coordinate and standardize their processes, they needed to identify and collect all documentation and describe the methods currently in use. A wide variety of external documents, such as medical codes, provider and Medicare handbooks, drug handbooks, and medical industry procedures, also had to be integrated into their final system.

HRM adopted a nuts-and-bolts approach to address the ISO process control requirements and at the same time support the ISO requirements for documentation and data. First, they asked people to identify the documents they currently used. They found employees were using a wide variety of support materials—claim forms, memos collected into three-ring binders, and even Post-It Notes®—to help them do their work. In order to bring order to both their processes and their documentation, HRM identified one individual who would be responsible to clear all documentation. They also worked together in cross-office teams to establish common practices for processes. These groups determined how they would handle both documentation and records, and how they would deal with their computer system. It took about a year of concentrated interaction between the offices in Kalamazoo and Minneapolis, but they found that they were able to smooth their operations and eliminate daily fire-fighting episodes that had been part of their organizational culture. Importantly, even with the need to expand their procedures to satisfy the ISO requirements, they discovered that they had less documentation than they had when they began their registration project.

LESSONS LEARNED

At the onset of their ISO registration project, Health Risk Management, Inc. decided to approach the core ideas of the standard as forming a very simple management system based on common sense. They perceived ISO as an approach to the basics of Management 101. Rather than attempting to focus on the sometimes fuzzy notion of quality, HRM focused on the more familiar notion of management. Perceiving the standard as elegant in its simplicity freed them to overcome several difficulties. First, this approach reduced the problem of trying to adapt the standard's manufacturing language to their service organization because focusing on the management ideas allowed them to see beyond the manufacturing terminology. Second, by focusing on the notion of commonsense management rather than on abstract procedures and quality, they were able to overcome the concern that writing procedures and controlling processes would hinder creativity and customer responsiveness. Essentially, HRM leveraged the ISO concepts to support their practical daily business outcomes.

14

ｰｼ ｒｰ

Section 4.10,
Inspection and Testing

THE KEY QUESTIONS

Section 4.10, Inspection and Testing, asks:

1. Do we know what we are supposed to do to receive products and services into our company, and are we doing it?
2. Do all our employees check their own work as they do it and before they pass it on to the next person along the service chain?
3. Before we finalize the service, do we know it is right?

INTERPRETING THE STANDARD

Of all the sections of the standard, this one most closely espouses the typical ideas of quality control. *Quality control* is an inspection activity—the idea is to inspect or to sample in order to discover errors or nonconformances. The ISO 9000 series, however, is based on the broader idea of *quality assurance,* which aims to control the processes and work flows that manufacture the product or produces the service and prevent nonconformances before they occur. Even if their processes are excellent, companies discover they must continue to ensure that individuals check their work as it passes through the process. In traditional manufacturing organizations, inspections typically are conducted during receiving inspections, at specified stop points during production, and in a final inspection before the product is released for shipment.

This section of the standard is divided into five subclauses. Each of these makes specific reference to conducting inspections and tests "in accordance with the quality plan and/or documented procedures." Typically ISO 9000 registrar auditors—in keeping with their traditional focus on manufacturing processes—expect to see well-defined and well-executed inspection and test activities at certain points in the manufacturing process. The purpose of these activities is "to verify that the specified requirements for the product are met." The final subclause requires records "which provide evidence that the product has been inspected and/or tested" as proof the product meets requirements and is ready for shipment to the customer. In addition to a procedure to describe the inspection and testing activities, the requirements in this section include:

- Incoming product not be used until inspected or otherwise "verified"
- The amount of control exercised over incoming product be based on the subcontractor's control or records of conformance
- If product is released for "urgent production purposes prior to verification," it must be identified so it can be recalled if subsequent inspection discovers a problem
- In-process inspections and requisite paperwork be completed at each step and before the product is released to the next step or phase of production
- A review to ensure all required inspections and tests have been completed is part of the final inspection step
- There are controls to ensure that product is not released until all inspections and tests—as well as required records as evidence—have been completed

There are some additional interesting notions in this section. First, the inspection and release authority—the individual or group who is authorized to release the product—must be identified in the quality plans or procedures. Also, if a product fails to pass an inspection, that fact must be duly recorded in the inspection documentation. This last requirement is new to the 1994 version of the standard—some registrars evidently were discovering that companies would inspect and fail a product and not include that information in the documentation. Finally, the section says that if a product fails an inspection, the requirements in Section 4.13, Control of Nonconforming Product, apply.

SERVICE PERSPECTIVES ON INSPECTION AND TESTING

Because frequently there is no physical product involved in the service activity, it might be tempting for you to skip this section in the mistaken belief that it does not apply to you. Not only is that an error that will short-change your quality program, it is unlikely to be accepted by your registrar. The process of inspection refers to both the product and to the process that produces the product or service. Your service organization does work with processes, and inspection and testing will help you assess those processes. For services, the inspection activity should focus at selected points in the process of providing the service to ensure that the work was done correctly and the results are satisfactory. If there is a tangible outcome as part of the service, that tangible outcome can be inspected for accuracy or against the customer's requirements. But—tangible output or not—service providers must examine the service processes as the work progresses.

There is an interesting and unusual variation in this section of the standard. Throughout the standard, the writers refer to the need to follow established procedures. However, in Section 4.10, Inspection and Testing, the writers refer both to the need to meet the requirements in relevant procedures and to the need to meet the requirements specified in the quality plans. In fact, the language "shall be in accordance with the quality plan and/or documented procedures" appears at least five times. The writers are emphasizing that plans should detail the steps in the process rather than the condition of the product. They are thus able to change the focus from an inspection process that examines just the product to an assessment that examines the process. This emphasis makes good sense to service providers. They can establish stop points or assessment points to ensure that the work in progress is being done properly, so the final outcomes will meet the customer's needs.

PRACTICAL EXAMPLES

- To *"ensure that incoming product is not used or processed . . . until it has been inspected or otherwise verified as conforming,"* the company clerk may conduct a receiving inspection of an office supplies order by checking the purchase order against the supplies received.

- To *"hold product until the required inspection and tests have been completed or necessary reports have been received and verified,"* a nurse may conduct an in-process inspection of samples collected from a patient to ensure that they are appropriately packaged and marked before they are sent to the laboratory for analysis.
- To ensure that *"no product shall be dispatched until all the activities specified . . . have been satisfactorily completed,"* a new car salesperson may review safety and operating procedures with the buyer as part of the delivery process to ensure that the customer is comfortable with the new car before it is released to the customer.
- To *"maintain records which provide evidence that the product has been inspected and/or tested,"* a human resources specialist may review all relevant paperwork for a newly hired employee to ensure that all steps in the hiring process have been completed.

COMPLYING WITH SECTION 4.10 IN SERVICE ORGANIZATIONS

Flowchart Work Flows and Processes

Service providers may have a good idea of what outcomes they hope to achieve for their customers, but may miss establishing some of the requisite steps to help their employees provide the service. A flowchart of the steps and outcomes will help identify not only what needs to be done, but also where redundancies, nonvalue-added steps, and bottlenecks may hinder efficient operations and frustrate both customers and service employees. A flowchart of the process, along with identified check or inspection points, will help organize the process and also help employees understand the natural stop points to ensure that they are making good progress toward their goals.

Identify the Stop Points

A stop point is a natural or obvious place in a process where employees can take a breath and look at where they are, what they have accomplished, and where they are going. In manufacturing or construction settings, a stop point is a completed task where an inspector ensures that all of the steps in the task have been completed successfully. Service providers can find natural stop points or inspection points when they flowchart a process and see the primary transitions between steps or groups of steps. The stop points allow and require service employees an opportunity to check their own work and catch errors before they become impossible to correct.

Find Value in Steps

Sometimes employees become so busy with the steps they must perform in order to meet deadlines or to service their customers that they lose sight of all of the steps it takes to complete a service transaction. Inspection or stop points mark the opportunities for employees to ensure that they are making good progress. The flowchart and stop or inspection points also provide everyone in the organization with an opportunity to understand the entire process and to think about ways to improve the efficiency and effectiveness of work flows.

CASE STUDY IN INSPECTION AND TESTING

Sally D'Angelo is the Manager of Client Services Support and ISO Management Representative for International Language Engineering (ILE) Corporation in Boulder, Colorado. The company has 240 employees in its Boulder corporate headquarters and in satellite offices in Santa Clara, California, and Boise, Idaho, as well as more than 800 contract translators working in more than 30 languages around the world. The company provides *localization* services for high-technology companies, particularly computer hardware and software manufacturers, medical equipment manufacturers, and pharmaceutical companies.

The term *localization* means that the company is able to take a product created in one country and prepare and translate it so that it appears that the product originally had been created in the translated-to language. Not only are there structural issues and differences among languages—such as different ways to express decimal numbers, date-time stamps, and currency—there are differences in word order and sentence structures. For example, sentences in many languages are longer than they are in English. Therefore, the size of computer help screens and dialogue boxes must be adjusted to accommodate the differences in sentence length. There are also subtle differences in the way languages express concepts and ideas. For example, case studies and examples used in training programs frequently will lose their meaning or effect when translated into another language. For the localization to be successful, the translation must not only change the words, length, and structure, but must also be sensitive to various country conventions, expressions, and concepts. A successful localization project is sensitive to the language structure and conventions, and ensures that the concepts are adequately translated so the ideas are completely and accurately expressed. This is especially important when dealing with high-tech products or health-related products, and is particularly difficult when dealing with medical and technical terms.

International Language Engineering Corporation's customers frequently include software development companies that provide specialized business applications worldwide. They localize software—including on-line and printed help screens, dialogue boxes the user sees, and program notes within the code the software developer sees—technical manuals, training manuals, and multimedia for software companies. Also, they localize operating and technical manuals for medical equipment manufacturers. Pharmaceutical companies use ILE's services for informational bulletins and care and use information. They work primarily with companies that see an opportunity for penetration into an overseas market. Thus, registration to ISO 9001 gives them an important marketing entry and means to support their customers more effectively.

Section 4.10, Inspection and Testing, gives ILE two advantages. First, it is an opportunity to inspect their work in progress, and second, it is an opportunity to make sure their processes are working properly. The process they use to translate and localize a project is highly iterative and has multiple check points where they can ensure that the project is progressing satisfactorily and the product they are producing is appropriate for their customer's needs. Briefly summarized, the steps include:

- The company prepares computer files containing the subject or information to be translated and sends that information, usually via ftp or electronic modem transmission, to the individual who will do the translation. The translator may be anywhere in the world, but most frequently is a native speaker in the country into which the product will be localized.

- The translator works—via electronic communication—with a translation coordinator and senior project manager at Boulder to arrive at an agreed-upon scope of work and time frame within which the work will be completed.
- The translator finishes the work and transmits it back to Boulder, where it is processed and formatted. The translation coordinator checks to make sure all files have been completed and returned and—for computer code translations—run correctly.
- The project manager or another translator at Boulder conducts a series of reviews, tests, and assessments to make sure the translation is correct and meets the company's quality standards. The terminology may be correct, but the assessor also looks at both the structure and content of the translation to ensure the understanding of concepts as well as words.
- The work is then transmitted to an editor of the native language who will read the material to make sure the original translator interpreted it such that a native reader will be able to understand the topic as written and the translation is useful for a native speaker.
- At this point the work will also go through a grammar and spell check, and, if required, a glossary of terms will be updated.
- Once these steps are completed, the work will go through a final processing step. For example, for a computer program translation, the ILE software engineers will bring up both the English and translated versions of the computer program on two separate computers and simultaneously take each program through every process routine, help menu, and dialogue box to make sure the program works correctly and all of the information is correctly translated.
- The project will go through another formatting and quality assurance check both at Boulder and in the country where it will be used to make sure it is correct and will work properly as designed.
- Usually there is one final step in which someone goes through the entire product to make sure the entire translation is correct before the product is released to the customer as completed.

The process of localizing a product from one language to another is a highly iterative undertaking with carefully defined check points along the way to ensure not only that the work is being done correctly, but also that the processes are effective and efficient. The company has numerous forms and check sheets to help guide the work of all participants in the process to ensure that each step is completed correctly. Also, the project manager works with a master schedule of steps or a tracking sheet that includes the requisite stop or inspection points. As each individual in the process completes her or his work and inspection of the work, the project manager keeps the project schedule updated so the company knows the project status as well as the inspection and test status of the project.

LESSONS LEARNED

International Language Engineering discovered several key lessons on their ISO journey. They recognized that while their service provides a tangible product, the fundamental nature of their service is the work and intelligence that goes into the localization activity to create the translated product. Their work is not like a batch of widgets that can be inspected and a bad batch can be returned. They must continuously monitor their work and catch and correct errors as early in the process as possible. ILE's inspection and testing activities are highly iterative to make sure they are on track and producing the best possible translation. Their definition of quality is to make the translated product as good as or better than the original-language version.

ILE also understood there would be a significant expenditure of resources to achieve registration. Although they had strong marketing reasons to achieve registration, particularly given the global nature of their business, they felt the marketing advantage was insufficient to make ISO valuable. Therefore, in order to justify registration, ILE sought to identify value-added outcomes ISO would bring to its processes. In addition to the advantage of helping them plan their work, their ISO project helped them look at all the steps along the way and to discover the points in the process where errors could occur and points in the process that would be natural stop points for them to inspect their work and catch errors early.

Because so much of their work is not done face-to-face—their translators are located worldwide—it is critical for everyone to understand all the steps, outcomes, and checkpoints so they can work together to complete their projects on time. The individual checklists and project tracking sheets help everyone understand their duties and responsibilities and identify the individual contributors as well as the promised milestones and delivery dates. The tracking sheets have also helped them eliminate nonvalue-added steps and improve the efficiency of the required steps.

Because ILE customer companies are leading-edge and high-technology companies, they find their lead times are always short and leave little room for slippage or delay. In fact, many software developers want to release their foreign-language versions of their programs simultaneously with the English-language version. As a result, ILE works with beta-level computer code and documentation right up until the last minute when they must finalize and release the product. Critical work, short lead times, and highly technical topics make it imperative that their work flows are lean, efficient, and without errors.

ILE's ISO registration also has provided a shift in focus. Sometimes ILE found itself under such time pressures to produce the work on schedule they were unable to see the overall process of the work and how each of the steps and the individual contributors worked together to complete the projects. Their registration has helped them see the overall process as well as the individual steps. In particular, the inspection and test section of the ISO standard has helped identify all of the points in the process where they need to stop and evaluate the work in order to provide a quality service.

15

⁓❧ ❦⁓

Section 4.11, Control of Inspection, Measuring, and Test Equipment

The Key Questions

Section 4.11, Control of Inspection, Measuring, and Test Equipment, asks:

1. Do we know what we need to measure, and do we have the measurement equipment we need to provide our service?
2. Do we know that our measurement equipment is capable of measuring what we want it to measure?
3. Do we know that our measurement equipment is accurately measuring what we think it is measuring; that is, is it properly calibrated?

Interpreting the Standard

In terms of length and detail, this section of the standard is the leader. Inspection, measuring, and test equipment (IMT) refers to anything used to measure or inspect product to ensure that it conforms to requirements—this includes test software. The standard spells out nine specific items you must cover in your IMT equipment procedure and program. Summarized, they require:

- A way to identify what needs to be measured and a way to select IMT equipment that can measure—to the accuracy needed—whatever is to be inspected or measured
- A complete list or record of all IMT equipment and a way to

identify IMT equipment used, including equipment owned by employees, and a program to calibrate each instrument at set intervals or prior to use

- A structured method to complete calibrations and to record that they have been completed
- Ways to protect equipment during calibrations—including controlling environmental conditions—during handling and storage, and protecting IMT from any mishandling from whatever source

SERVICE PERSPECTIVES ON IMT EQUIPMENT

Inspection, measuring, and test equipment can be as simple as a clock on the wall or as complex as the software used to ensure that a complex piece of machinery is functioning properly on a spacecraft. Most registrars will not ask companies to calibrate their office clocks unless they serve as time clocks or are used for precise measures of performance. In traditional manufacturing environments, IMT equipment includes scales, gages, meters, and software to control machinery. In high-technology and new technology areas—especially those in which new materials are developed—it is necessary not only to invent new IMT equipment, but also to devise ways to calibrate it.

This section on IMT equipment is related to Section 4.20, Statistical Techniques; it asks you to focus on the measurement device itself, rather than on its application or on the statistical tools applied to the measurement results. You use IMT to gather the numbers, and you use statistical techniques to make sense of the resulting data. Service organizations, particularly those that have adopted quality initiatives, understand the value of using statistical techniques as part of their self-evaluation process as well as to measure daily activities. These statistical tools and self-evaluation activities typically are addressed in Section 4.20, Statistical Techniques.

For service organizations, some examples of inspection, measuring, and testing equipment are:

- A typing test, which is a measurement device used to hire a new clerk
- A checklist used to instruct an individual on how to perform a

task, which is then used as a measurement device to demonstrate skill acquisition
- Supervisors monitoring telephone calls and assessing them to ensure quality service
- Measuring employees' performance for speed, accuracy, and for qualitative attributes such as friendliness all require a yardstick of some type, and so fall into the category of IMT equipment

For your service organization, the first part of this section of the standard requires you to understand what you need to measure and to select measuring devices capable of providing the desired outcome. The second part of the section identifies nine areas of concern you should consider and include in your procedure on IMT equipment. The nine areas are spelled out in detail as subclauses 4.11.2 a through i.

PRACTICAL EXAMPLES

- To *"determine the measurements to be made and the accuracy required,"* a jeweler/assayer may select weighing scales that can be calibrated in order to guarantee customers that weights are accurate within one one-hundredth of an ounce.
- In order to *"demonstrate the conformance of the product to specified requirements,"* a personnel payroll company may provide accurate time clocks to customers as part of its service.
- To identify equipment *"with a suitable indicator or approved identification record,"* a state truck inspection authority may calibrate its scales daily and display a record of that event so interstate trucks are accurately weighted and within the established regulated limits.
- To *"select the appropriate . . . equipment . . . capable of the necessary accuracy and precision,"* a human resources manager may select a psychological profile test for new hires based on the test's known validity to measure what it says it measures.

COMPLYING WITH SECTION 4.11 IN SERVICE ORGANIZATIONS

Use Outside Agencies

Unless your company is a large laboratory or you have fairly sophisticated equipment, it is probably significantly less expensive and troublesome to subcontract IMT equipment calibration to a qualified vendor(s). Calibration service providers are very expensive, but in comparison to performing these tasks in-house, they generally represent a cost-effective way to accomplish the tasks.

Make Your Program Useful to Your Needs

Laboratories and other industries that rely heavily on IMT equipment have fairly stringent guidelines and requirements established by either regulatory or industry agencies. That is not the case for many service organizations. Your IMT equipment program is yours to design to fit your needs. You must decide what to measure and what degree of accuracy you want and need to satisfy your customer. You also must determine how frequently to calibrate IMT equipment based on your experience with it as well as your needs.

CASE STUDY IN IMT EQUIPMENT

Snelling Personnel Services in Tampa, Florida, is registered to ISO 9002. The seven-person company, begun in 1988, is the only one of 400 national franchisees in the Snelling system registered to ISO. Tampa is not a manufacturing center, and this is reflected in the kinds of temporary and contract staffing provided by the office. About 50 percent of this office's business is long-term, with contracts of a year or more. Most contracts and most assignments are for high-end office and clerical, word processing, and administrative assistants, as well as accounting and data processing personnel. Snelling also provides computer programmers, technical writers, and information systems professionals.

President Don Hurd and Management Representative Wanda Petkiewicz worked with a consultant to achieve registration. Their inspiration for ISO came when they were getting ready to go through a vendor recertification with one of their major clients. The client, who is ISO-registered, asked them if they were registered as well. The customer was trying to reduce its vendor base to fewer than 100 subcontractors, and Don saw ISO as one way to help keep his company on his customer's short list. The effort has paid off. In addition, Snelling is seeing increasingly frequent requests for quotes (RFQs) that ask, "Are you registered to ISO?" as part of the qualification process.

When Don and his team started thinking about how to apply the requirements of IMT equipment to their work processes, they realized that one of the primary issues for the success of their business was making sure there is a good match between the contract employee's skills and what the customer requires. They use two primary tactics to ensure a good match. First, they use computerized testing for such things as typing and other basic skills. This test is provided by a software developer who is itself ISO-registered, so communication was easy between Snelling and the software provider, who understood Don's concerns and needs. As in all IMT equipment situations, the first question is "Do we know what we need to measure, and can this measurement instrument give us what we need?" The computer system is moderately elaborate and has safeguards to make sure candidates cannot influence the scores to make their performance appear better than their skills. This helps satisfy the requirements of Section 4.11.2, which says companies must take precautions that "safeguard . . . from adjustments which would invalidate the calibration setting."

An important issue affecting how this company approached IMT is that candidate test performance is not necessarily a pass-fail situation—the test is specific and diagnostic. The tests must be valid—that is, they measure what they are supposed to measure—and they must help the staff appropriately match candidates to assignments. Snelling uses an additional tactic to address this issue—taking advantage of feedback from the customer. When they receive a request for a temporary person, they carefully determine from a detailed checklist what specific skills the customer is looking for, and candidates are tested on the computer system for those skills. Although it might have been possible to describe this tactic within the requirements of Section 4.20, Statistical Techniques, Don and Wanda believed that, given its purpose, the issue was better handled under IMT equipment.

Their IMT process does not stop there, however. They involve their customers in the process of checking to see if the IMT equipment is, in fact, "capable of verifying the acceptability of product," and they further recheck at prescribed intervals, as the standard requires. To do this, they place calls to the customer on the first day to make sure the new employee arrived on schedule, and on the second day to ensure that all is well. At the end of a short-term assignment, they ask customers to complete a detailed assessment of the temporary employee's performance. During long-term assignments, they make periodic calls to ensure that the temporary personnel continue to meet the client's needs, or if there needs to be an adjustment.

LESSONS LEARNED

It is deceptively easy to assume that a particular piece of testing equipment is appropriate or useful for the assessment or performance measure it claims to make. Snelling went beyond this assumption and did several things particularly well in describing the IMT procedures for their ISO registration. First, they were creative in considering how the section could be useful to their needs. Because they also used software from an ISO-registered company, they did not need to calibrate the software for their use, but were able to rely on the software provider to assure that the programs are appropriately calibrated. Additionally, Snelling successfully tied this section into their basic work processes of selecting and placing contract employees. And, finally, they directly involved customers as participants to help satisfy the requirements of this section of the standard while at the same time ensuring they are satisfying customer needs.

The language of ISO and the processes recommended in its requirements are sometimes a challenge to both understanding and application in service settings, and many service companies believe they have little reason to consider this section of the standard. Although addressing these issues through the requirements of Section 4.20, Statistical Techniques, is one tactic, it is important to remember that statistical techniques address the process of evaluating, whereas IMT equipment looks at the efficacy of the tools used to conduct the assessment.

16

꜄ ꜅

Section 4.12,
Inspection and Test Status

THE KEY QUESTIONS

Section 4.12, Inspection and Test Status, asks:

1. Have we carefully thought through the steps necessary to provide the service and identified planned stop points to ensure that the work is being completed satisfactorily?
2. Do we know if one step in our service process has been completed and/or inspected as correct before we begin the next step in the process?

INTERPRETING THE STANDARD

Section 4.8, Product Identification and Traceability, establishes requirements to identify individual products. For physical products, that usually means using part numbers or serial numbers on individual components, subassemblies, or finished products. Section 4.12, Inspection and Test Status, is somewhat similar to Section 4.8 in that it requires the company to identify the current condition of the product in terms of the inspection requirements identified in the quality plan or procedures. Usually, most companies have established three grades or conditions to classify their products in terms of inspection. These classifications are: waiting inspection; inspected and passed; inspected and failed, or nonconforming. Some companies use a two status category system: inspected/passed or noncon-

forming. These companies see both product that has failed and unin-
spected product as nonconforming.

This section requires that the status be maintained throughout
the entire production cycle. This does not mean inspected product
must be labeled or marked, but that is a frequent solution to fulfill-
ing this requirement. One way to identify product that has not
passed inspections—and this is in keeping with the requirements of
Section 4.13, Control of Nonconforming Product—is to segregate it
into a special, marked area, or to dispose of it in marked containers.
Essentially, this section of the standard is designed to make sure the
company always knows the current inspection status—has it been
inspected, has it passed the inspection—of all products produced
and to ensure that nonconforming product is not allowed to continue through the process or to be shipped to the customer.

SERVICE PERSPECTIVES ON INSPECTION AND TEST STATUS

Service companies easily can use this section of the standard as
part of their control processes and to understand their service cycle.
It is particularly useful, along with Section 4.10, Inspection and
Testing, to determine the progress and completion of services provided. Inspections often require the service provider or individual
performing the tasks to stop and determine how well the job has
progressed so far. These stop points are usually identified in the
production or service plan under Section 4.2.3, Quality Planning.
The requirements to identify the status strengthens and contributes
to the motivation to identify the stop points in the service planning
stages and to complete the inspections during the execution of the
service. Planned stop points clearly signal an expectation to the
individual performing the task that he or she should conduct an
inspection at that point before proceeding. Inspection status is a visible marker the inspections have been done.

PRACTICAL EXAMPLES

- To identify the *"test status of product . . . by suitable means,"* a
  blood laboratory may use a permanent marker to label collected blood donations as having passed lab tests for contami-
  nation.
- To identify *"throughout production, installation, and servicing,"* an

auto rental company may park cars in a designated area to indicate they have been inspected and need mechanical repair.

- To ensure product *"has passed the required inspections"* before it is *"dispatched, used, or installed,"* a hotel housekeeper clears the key lock to indicate a room is now available to be rented to a new guest.

COMPLYING WITH SECTION 4.12 IN SERVICE ORGANIZATIONS

Link to Section 4.2.3, Quality Planning, and 4.10, Inspection and Testing

The planning and inspection activities help keep processes in control and thereby support service providers' efforts to achieve their desired and expected goals. The relationship among process planning, status activities, and inspections is an important one. Status activities provide a visible way to ensure that planning and inspections are operating effectively. The links form an important means to let individuals providing the service understand what is expected of them and give them a way to measure their own performance by being able to track the current status of their work.

Keep the Markers Simple

Status markers must be simple. Color tags, easily pasted-on labels, any kind of easy-to-apply marker, and simple geography can all be used as ways to indicate inspection status. The markers should be both simple and obvious. For example, the classic In-Out boxes on a desk are clear and simple markers of the status of the work being completed. Similarly, inspection markers will help control the flow of work. Complex markers or status identifiers that slow down the worker or cause delays in providing the service not only hinder the efficient delivery of the service, they demoralize workers and reduce their willingness to provide a good service.

Use Markers as Performance Feedback

In even the most effective companies, most employees report that they do not get enough feedback on their performance. But not all feedback is a verbal response from a supervisor. One effective way to get performance feedback is from the task itself, in this case from the satisfying action of completing a task and marking it finished or ready for the next step. Training employees and supervisors to recognize status markers as immediate feedback and material for regular verbal feedback is another benefit of this section.

Case Study in Inspection and Test Status

Charles River Saab is the oldest Saab dealer in the United States, and the first auto dealer in the U.S. to achieve registration to ISO 9000. They sought registration for several reasons. First, their market territory is highly competitive, not only among the ten Saab dealerships in the greater Boston metropolitan area, but also with other imports, including Audi, BMW, Lexus, and Volvo. Second, because there are many high-technology and international companies in their market area, their customers have heard about and understand the concepts underlying ISO registration. Third, their clientele tend to be highly educated and exceptionally well-informed, as well as extremely quality conscious. Finally, automobile customers everywhere are particularly concerned about the quality and reputation of maintenance and service repair organizations. According to June Peckingham, their ISO Management Representative, Charles River Saab sees its ISO registration as one way to distinguish itself from their competition and to offer their customers an external validation of the quality of their service.

Charles River Saab is the first automobile dealership in the United States to achieve registration; however, they are by no means the first in the automobile industry to achieve compliance and registration against a quality standard. The Big Three U.S. automobile makers—Ford, GM, and Chrysler—along with several truck manufacturers, have created the QS-9000 standard and are requiring their suppliers to seek and achieve registration to this standard. Championed by the Automotive Industry Action Group (AIAG), QS-9000 begins with the exact language of all of the 20 sections of the ISO standard. Then each section includes additional requirements particular to the automotive industry. Finally, there are several additional sections to the QS standard that address the needs and expectations of each of the Big Three.

Although QS-9000 has become a requirement for many suppliers to the automotive industry, the requirements do not include car dealerships, which are customers of the automakers. Felix Bosshard, the President of Charles River Saab, is from Europe, where he has seen the value of ISO registration as a strategic business issue. Felix thought that, in addition to distinguishing the dealership among his customers, seeking ISO registration would allow his company to be one step ahead if the automakers decided to request registration from their dealers.

Registration also provided the dealership with some internal support of several quality initiatives they had underway, particularly in the service areas. Most of the 50 employees at the dealership work in the service area. They employ five service advisors, 14 service technicians and seven parts department personnel. As part of a quality initiative, the service department had formed teams to ensure that the best qualified persons were assigned to particular tasks. The team concept helps ensure excellent service, but requires extraordinary cooperation and communication among the team members, several of whom may work on one customer's automobile. Each team member must inspect his own work before passing the car to the next service technician. Obviously, the inspection and test status of each repair task must be identified if the team service process is to work well.

Inspection and Test Status is important in several tasks in the service process, including receipt of new automobiles into stock from the distributor, preparation of new cars for delivery to purchasers, and service and repair of customers' cars. In all three areas, Charles River Saab uses both a computer-based and a paper indicator to show the current inspection and test status of individual automobiles. When a new auto is received into stock, both a paper check-in form and a computer repair order are generated. The paper checklist stays in the car until the inspection has been completed and serves as a visual indication of its inspection and test status. The paperwork also serves as a checklist of all of the items that must be attended to in order to receive the automobile into stock. Similarly, when a new automobile is sold, both a computer-based inspection order and a paper checklist are generated by the service department. The checklist guides the service technician through the final inspection before delivery, and the salesperson uses the record to review the order with the customer as part of the delivery process.

Computer- and paper-based repair orders also are used by the service department staff for maintenance and repair of customer automobiles. The inspection and test status is noted in both formats by the technician who works on the auto and by the service advisor so that its inspection and test status is known as the car is worked on by different members of the team. Also, as part of satisfying the ISO 9000 status requirements, they have a special marking on the key tag and service order for patrons who elect to wait in the dealership for their car service work to be completed. In all of these situations the checklists help ensure that all important safety checks are completed, including road tests, and little details such as topping off fluids are attended to.

LESSONS LEARNED

ISO registration has provided Charles River Saab several advantages. In addition to its marketing value among its savvy customers, the dealership has been able to gain value by coordinating several of the ISO requirements to support their routine activities. For example, they have integrated their procedures for Inspection and Test Status (Section 4.12), Quality Planning (Section 4.2.3), and Inspection and Testing (Section 4.10) to operate as a whole to serve their needs. According to June Peckingham, Charles River Saab wants to do more than just make their customers happy. It is vitally important they prevent errors and problems from recurring. Their procedures have helped them to plan and streamline their processes and keep everyone informed. Their ISO program, including its internal audit program, helps keep everyone on their toes, working and communicating together to provide an excellent service. The net results are satisfied customers who return to Charles River Saab for maintenance and repair, and when they decide to purchase a new automobile.

17

⁓⤳ ⤳⁓

Section 4.13, Control of Nonconforming Product

THE KEY QUESTIONS

Section 4.13, Control of Nonconforming Product, asks:

1. If something is wrong, do we take necessary steps to make sure the error does not continue through the work process and, further, make sure it does not go to the customer?
2. Do we: identify; document; evaluate; segregate; dispose of; and notify persons affected when we have a failure?

INTERPRETING THE STANDARD

In addition to the goal of satisfying customers, a basic tenet of ISO 9000 is to eliminate nonconformances or waste in processes. A quality management system is designed to control manufacturing or service processes. When these processes are in control, then a quality product or service should result. The notion of total quality control or zero defects focuses on establishing a system that prevents errors. The ISO standard adopts a more pragmatic view, acknowledging that some errors are likely to be made and nonconformances are likely to be generated. Section 4.13, Control of Nonconforming Product, helps companies structure a way to control nonconformances so they do not slip through the system and reach the customer, or in the language of the standard, are "prevented from unintended use or installation."

145

In addition to requiring a procedure, the standard requires companies to establish a six-step process for dealing with nonconforming products. The six steps look like a generic problem-solving flowchart. The six steps are to identify, document, evaluate, segregate (when practical), dispose, and notify other organizational functions that may be affected.

To deal with nonconforming product, the standard suggests four possible resolutions. These are not the only ways to deal with nonconforming product, but most resolutions probably fit into one of the four. They are:

- Rework the product to meet the requirements
- Ask the customer to accept—with concession—the product with or without repair
- Regrade the product for an alternative application
- Reject or scrap the product

If there is a contractual agreement with the customer covering nonconforming product, the standard additionally requires the company to report nonconformances to the customer for concession and provide a record denoting the actual condition of the product.

The standard does not suggest that the customer be asked to accept the product without repair and without concession. If the product is reworked, the standard stipulates an interesting requirement. It requires the reworked product to be reinspected according to the quality plans or procedures. It would seem logical to reinspect a reworked product, but evidently this is not always true. The writers of the standard felt compelled to add this provision.

SERVICE PERSPECTIVES ON CONTROL OF NONCONFORMING PRODUCT

At first, some service providers might think this section is not relevant to them, because of the word *product* in the title. However, the term *product* in ISO terminology includes service activities. Both products and services are the result of a series of steps and activities that provide a value-added deliverable to the customer. Therefore, service providers should consider their service as a product.

Addressing the requirements in this section of the standard will be useful to their quality management program.

Service companies are at a certain disadvantage when dealing with control of nonconforming product. Manufactured products are tangible, and producers have an opportunity to inspect for non-conformances before they reach the customer. In contrast, service providers frequently do not have the opportunity to catch and control errors before they reach the customer. In these cases, the company must correct the failure with the customer's knowledge, or apologize to the customer for the error. The standard's stipulation to "prevent from unintended use or installation" is not met once the customer has become involved in the problem. Such a failure or nonconforming product, at best, reduces the customer's confidence or, at worse, angers the customer who then becomes a negative advertiser of the company.

There is copious evidence that individuals who have good experiences with a company will tell one friend or colleague, whereas an individual who has a bad or disappointing experience with a company will report it to eight friends or colleagues. The challenge is, primarily, to prevent errors, or if they occur, to control them. ISO Section 4.9, Process Control, deals with ensuring that customers always receive the expected service without error. Section 4.13, Control of Noncomforming Product, addresses actions to take if an error occurs.

The first task for any service provider in establishing procedures to deal with errors is to develop a list of potential breakdowns in processes or failures. For example, some types of service providers have difficulty meeting on-time requirements, such as when a service technician is delayed on a job with one customer and therefore is late arriving at a second appointment. Other time delays include long lines in a bank that keep customers waiting for service, or an airline flight delayed because of mechanical or weather difficulties. Other difficulties include service providers providing wrong information or improperly processing an activity for a customer. For example, a ticket clerk at the movie theater may tell a patron the wrong start time for a feature film, or a waitress may charge the wrong amount for a meal.

Once as many as possible of the potential problem areas are identified, the company should establish methods to handle the most likely of them. This does not mean the company should consider every potential problem that could conceivably ever occur. However, problems susceptible to error or likely to occur should be identified, and a set of responses to these failures should be identified. For example, if a scheduled flight is delayed or canceled, airlines will arrange for alternative transportation and accommodations for passengers in local hotels. A different response is in order when severe weather closes airports and many people are stranded.

Identifying potential nonconformances and developing contingency plans to deal with them will give employees structured guidelines to enable them to respond to customers when nonconformances occur. It is not necessary to develop detailed responses to each specific kind of incident. However, general guidelines within categories of contingencies will support front-line employees by giving them ways to think about responses to nonconformances. Customers will be less frustrated with breakdowns or service failures if they see the service employee is able to deal successfully and quickly with the problem. Leaving an employee without adequate guidance to deal with nonconformances not only frustrates the employee, but also sends a clear signal to customers that the company doesn't care about its customers or is unable to provide the promised service.

In addition to determining potential nonconformances, the service company also should use appropriate statistical metrics to track failures and breakdowns in the services it provides. These data can help the company not only improve their processes to eliminate breakdowns, but also give them established contingency plans when errors occur.

PRACTICAL EXAMPLES

- To *"ensure that product that does not conform to specified requirements is prevented from unintended use,"* an emergency medical technician ambulance driver may conduct monthly checks of disposable medical supplies to ensure that they have not deteriorated or become unfit for use.
- To be *"regraded for alternative applications,"* a hotel clerk may

offer a guest a free upgrade to a better room if the room originally booked is not ready for occupancy.

- To provide *"notification to the functions concerned,"* an electric utility may notify customers that service will be interrupted for scheduled repairs.

COMPLYING WITH SECTION 4.13 IN SERVICE ORGANIZATIONS

Identify the Product

Service products are in many cases actually an accumulation of features and value-added elements. Thus, whereas identifying the product may seem obvious, unraveling the source of errors or nonconforming product can be complex. Because the service frequently is not a single entity, several kinds of failures can degrade the total service experience or interaction. In addition, some aspects of the service are more important to the customer than others. Service providers therefore must be prepared to recover from and correct all the individual aspects of the total service experience.

Rely on Metrics

Collecting various metrics related to service interruptions, breakdowns, and failures will help you develop contingency plans to deal with problems that reach the customer. These metrics also will identify trends and support problem-solving activities to help you conduct root-cause analyses of problems in order to find their solution.

Identify the Problem, Not the Product

The standard requires service companies to identify, document, evaluate, segregate (when practical), dispose of, and notify concerned functions. In manufacturing settings, these six steps refer to the tangible product. Service providers would not necessarily want to follow them all—segregation and disposal of the customer are not likely to be applicable. However, service companies are in a position to notify other members of the service organization of the needed changes and, further, notify the customer that the service failure has been corrected. Service providers should closely tie their continuous improvement programs or corrective and preventive action programs to their control of nonconforming product program.

CASE STUDY IN CONTROL OF NONCONFORMING PRODUCT

The chemical laboratory at PPG Industries' Lake Charles facility is independently registered to ISO 9002. The chemical laboratory provides analytical and technical support to the Lake Charles plant which produces commodity chemicals such as sodium hydroxide, chlorine, and chlorinated derivatives. Paper manufacturers use caustic soda, municipalities use chlorine to treat municipal water systems, plastics makers use the derivatives, and solvents are used in metal manufacturing stamping and drilling. Aerospace companies use their chemical products to clean fuel lines and other lines that need to be oil free. PPG Lake Charles also provides solvents to clean movie film. The lab provides analyses of finished chemicals produced by the plant and of raw materials received into the plant from vendors.

The chemical lab provides lab analyses and related services for chemical business units internal to PPG. There are about 50 employees in the lab serving 1600 people at the Lake Charles location. They also provide quality control and maintenance for several small laboratories in the various individual PPG production units and help the companies that provide terminal services monitor some small external companies that sell to PPG. Further, the lab may do some development and project chemist work to address specific problems. However, they are not a research lab, and all of their work is related to practical applications and problem solving. In addition to the ISO 9000 standards, the lab also supports compliance to environmental standards and both company-mandated and government-related requirements.

According to Beverly Schalon, the lab's ISO and Quality Assurance Coordinator, PPG made a corporate decision in the late 1980s that all business units within the corporation should begin the process for seeking registration. Every time one of the corporation's business units was about to be registered, the registrar would identify the analytical services provided by the chemical laboratory as integral and define the laboratory as a primary service provider to the business unit. Therefore, the registrar would want to include the chemical lab as part of each audit. As a result, the laboratory decided to seek independent ISO registration to allow the other business units to be able to say they have an ISO-registered lab doing their work for them. The result helped the business units and eliminated redundant audits at the chemical laboratory.

When the chemical lab began to address the nonconforming product issue, their first priority was to define their product. They determined that the nature of their service was really two-fold. First, because the activity they performed was the analysis of chemical samples, it was possible to see this activity as the service. However, from the main plant's perspective, the real service was the data that the laboratory provided to it. Nonconforming product became defined as any data that did not fall within the expected parameters of data obtained from the analysis.

There are essentially two reasons why the data would fall outside of the expected parameters. First, the sample might show a problem with the plant's produced chemical or a vendor-supplied chemical (true positive). Second, there might be a problem with the way the lab analysis was performed (false positive). For materials received into the plant that fail the analysis, the lab works with the shipping and receiving department to handle the product much as any manufacturing organization would. They identify and segregate the incoming product and usually will return it or dispose of it appropriately. For analysis performed on plant-produced products, the chemical lab also will look at its analysis processes and its own samples to ensure that the data that they have generated is correct.

The chemical laboratory has established quality assurance (QA) samples for all their products. Some of these QA samples are standards prepared in-house and traceable to the NIST. Others are control samples that have been analyzed repeatedly over a period of time to establish their "true" value. In all cases the lab has a series of QA protocols. Statistical process control charts are used to identify problems within the system. If the lab does not get the expected result from an analysis, they analyze a QA sample to verify the status of the test, re-analyze the sample or notify the plant, depending on the situation and applicable protocol.

Several possible causes might generate unanticipated data results. The sample from the plant may in fact be bad (positive-positive). A reagent used in the test may have gone bad. A measurement instrument may have slipped out of calibration. There could be a calculation error or an error in the way the lab test was performed. In all cases, corrective action is taken to determine the cause and to rectify the problem. Once the lab has determined that their processes are correct and that the data analysis shows a problem with the sample rather than with the way the analysis was done, the lab will ask the plant to investigate to determine its cause.

LESSONS LEARNED

The PPG Lake Charles Laboratory recently successfully completed their triennial audit and re-registration. In these three years, they have learned several important lessons. First, they discovered the value of ISO in helping them improve their processes. They saw registration as a hook that would help them achieve this. Because of the fundamental nature and activities of their business, conducting lab analyses, they are very process-oriented. They are also very quality-oriented in how they do their work, the way they handle their processes, and the way they serve their customers. Achieving ISO registration became a matter of pride for the individuals at the Chemical Laboratory.

Second, ISO registration has helped them keep documentation up to date through process changes. Because of the nature of their work, they are comfortable with using procedures and work instructions. Like many companies, however, keeping the documentation up to date was a challenge. They developed a simple process to update their documentation, and their registration has motivated them to keep their documents current. They learned much from the registrar auditors about how to look at processes, and how to assess and improve those processes.

Third, they were able to use ISO's internal audit processes and the extrinsic evaluation of registration and surveillance audits as a way to provide tangible evidence to their own staff that they are doing a good job. It also demonstrates to customers that they are providing a high quality service. During their triennial audit they received no nonconformances, which is strong evidence that they are doing an excellent job. Finally, by identifying their data as the primary feature of their service, the lab was able to use the ISO standard to focus their response to problems on how to handle nonconforming product.

18

❧ ❦

Section 4.14, Corrective and Preventive Action

THE KEY QUESTIONS

Section 4.14, Corrective and Preventive Action, asks:

1. When something is identified as wrong, does the individual responsible make sure the problem is resolved?
2. Do we effectively and efficiently handle customer complaints and comments?

INTERPRETING THE STANDARD

Corrective and Preventive Action (CPA) is the ISO equivalent to total quality management's idea of continuous improvement. It requires a procedure to describe an efficient program for corrective and preventive action. It further requires the approaches and solutions chosen to be consistent with the magnitude of the identified problems and opportunities for improvement. The wording in this section states the solutions to problems should be "to a degree appropriate to the magnitude of problems and commensurate with the risks encountered." Simply put, don't hit a fly with a sledge hammer.

The section is divided into two parts, corrective action and preventive action. *Corrective actions* are taken when you have identified a problem. *Preventive actions* anticipate the potential for future problems. It is important to note that the requirement for preventive action is new to the 1994 edition of the standard. The previous version (1987) required only corrective actions. Unfortunately, many companies interpreted this as requiring them only to quick-fix problems. The addition of preventive action was ISO's response to the need for continuous improvement. It requires companies to gather data in order to predict and prevent potential problems.

Preventive action strengthens the requirements of this section and requires the company to look deeper into the causes of potential problems. The requirements for both preventive and corrective action are essentially the same. In addition to handling customer complaints effectively and updating documented procedures in response to changes, in both cases the standard requires:

- Use of appropriate sources of data to generate information to assess the magnitude of risk
- Investigation of the cause(s) of problems
- Determination of a solution(s) to resolve the problem
- Follow-up controls to assess the effectiveness of the solution
- In all cases, response to customer complaints

In addition, the preventive action subsection requires that reports on preventive actions taken be incorporated into the management review process required in Section 4.1, Management Responsibility. Although not required by the standard, it is good practice to also report on corrective actions as part of management review.

SERVICE PERSPECTIVES ON CORRECTIVE AND PREVENTIVE ACTION

Corrective and Preventive Action is one of the three basic components of a good ISO quality assurance program. The other key components are Internal Quality Audits (Section 4.17) and Management Review (Section 4.1.3). Essentially, if the service organization personnel are looking at their own processes and procedures (internal audits) and identifying problems and taking advantage of opportunities for improvement (corrective/preventive action) and if management is supporting these efforts (management review), then you probably have a framework within which a good ISO 9000 quality management program will operate.

Service organizations should have an easier time with this requirement than traditional manufacturing organizations. Manufacturers often tend to focus on systems and machines and outputs rather than on people. In contrast, service companies routinely deal with people and assuring that customers are satisfied with their interactions with the company. Basic people skills are a solid foundation for a good corrective and preventive action program. Unlike manufacturers who send a product to a customer, service providers usually have direct face-to-face contact with the ultimate customer and must interact in a one-on-one setting to successfully provide the customer with the service.

Service organizations may fall into a trap if they fail to focus on the difference between corrective actions and preventive actions. Fixing problems or apologizing to customers when there is an error represents a corrective action. Good customer service, however, is more than responding to customer complaints. It is creating an environment in which customer complaints are avoided. In fact, good service should be invisible. That is, there should never be a problem that causes the customer to complain. Preventive actions, which result from the ability to foresee and avoid potential problems, is at the heart of a good continuous improvement and preventive action program.

Any structured, disciplined problem-solving methodology can be adapted to serve your corrective and preventive action program. Usually the steps in such a structured program are to:

- Identify an issue
- Gather and analyze data to learn the magnitude of the issue
- Identify and solicit inputs from affected stakeholders
- Develop a variety of alternative solutions
- Evaluate various solutions based on predetermined criteria and select the best
- Gain management and budget approval to implement the selected solution
- Implement the solution and verify its effectiveness
- Notify all stakeholders and update necessary procedures and work instructions

PRACTICAL EXAMPLES

- To provide for *"effective handling of customer complaints and reports of product nonconformities,"* an airline may have an office to deal with lost luggage.

- To use *"appropriate sources of information,"* an advertising agency may use focus groups and market research to determine which facets of a company's service are seen by the customer as least satisfactory.
- To *"ensure that corrective action is taken and that it is effective,"* an auto dealership may telephone service department customers who returned dissatisfied or needing additional repairs to their automobiles.

COMPLYING WITH SECTION 4.14 IN SERVICE ORGANIZATIONS

Use Existing Strengths

There is no need to reinvent the wheel. Many companies have programs, talents, and experiences they can easily fold into their corrective and preventive action program. Such things as problem-solving techniques, team-based improvement processes, quality tools, and other quality initiatives are useful foundations on which to build an effective ISO corrective and preventive action program.

Use Multiple Inputs

The standard focuses on customer complaints and refers to non-conformances. Some companies misinterpret the language to limit the CPA program to fixing nonconformances identified in audits and responding to customer complaints. That approach is short-sighted. A wide variety of inputs can be used to identify opportunities for improvement. Engineering change requests, focus groups, employee suggestions, returns, waste reports, late and supplemental shipment reports, and all other performance data provide a wealth of information and are all grist for your corrective and preventive action mill.

Track Program Administration

Half the battle simply is tracking administrative issues through to resolution. Too frequently, problems slip through the cracks, and solutions therefore are delayed. You do not need a major administrative structure to track your corrective and preventive action program; however, you must make sure problems are not allowed to fester or remain unresolved. You do need to make sure corrective and preventive actions are a routine and ongoing part of the daily attention given by management.

Tread Softly

Identifying issues, problems, errors, and fumbles can be easily misinterpreted as criticism and blame. You are not the local constabulary. Your job is not to seek out and punish the guilty. ISO looks at the process that accomplishes the work, and you should make sure your corrective and preventive action program focuses on process issues, not on personnel or disciplinary issues. If there is a personnel problem, use your human resources program, not your ISO program, to resolve it. That's what the HR program is for and you will protect your ISO program from being perceived as a management hammer.

CASE STUDY IN CORRECTIVE AND PREVENTIVE ACTION

Becky Harper was the Programs and Planning Manager, as well as the Quality Management Representative, for Apple America's Customer Support Center in Austin, Texas. The center's service consists of taking and processing orders, managing customers' accounts, providing pre-sales and new product information, and providing configuration and data enabling customers to make a purchase decision.

The Austin support center started their ISO project in 1994 when few service companies were seeking registration, so they had few models and experiences to draw on. Apple Computer saw registration, in part, as a research project to identify the potential and future direction of their company rather than just as a response to customer requirements. They also saw ISO registration as one way to grow their organization strategically. The Austin Center was to establish a model for a higher standard of performance that other non-manufacturing groups within the company could match.

The 450 people working in Austin are part of a matrix organization interlinked with other Apple corporate functions, including purchasing and manufacturing. Corrective and preventive action requirements—especially preventive action—added a challenge to the Austin service center. They discovered many of the root-causes for problems they were handling originated outside their own sphere of control. That is, Austin found itself dealing with customer complaints for problems which they could do little to prevent.

One significant challenge was the problem of identifying and clarifying the limits of accountability and responsibility for various internal and external functions within the corporation. Part of the success of their preventive and corrective action program was finding a way to track and escalate issues, particularly to establish processes to escalate nonconformance issues outside the Austin center. Their CPA program helps them with internal issues, and they have succeeded in using this requirement of the standard to help align communications between themselves and other groups within the company.

In another example, the Customer Support Center used their corrective and preventive action program to help provide feedback to the sales programs, as well as to promotions and marketing efforts. Austin now does a postmortem on all promotions, looking for ways to avoid elements that reduce profitability due to excessive expenses. On paper, a promotion may appear profitable, but such things as work-around solutions, increased customer tracking, and additional expenses incurred for air shipments subtract value from the process and reduce gross margins. Before ISO, marketing persons thought a promotion was a success when it appeared to make a lot of sales and seemed to satisfy the customer. Now, the Austin center is using its CPA program to provide data and visibility on program profitability to various functions within the organization, so the company can use this postmortem program to assess profitability. An executive summary helps executive management and marketing personnel look at issues and lessons learned to help develop future promotions while trying to avoid potential problems.

LESSONS LEARNED

Cross-functional communication and cooperation issues can be coordinated in a variety of ways within the ISO 9000 rubric. For example, it is possible to use Section 4.20, Statistical Techniques, as one way to share data and information. At first, the Austin group would send out a report of problems encountered and try to make sure management followed up. However, they learned that the more people and departments you send data and problems to, the fewer people feel responsible for the problem. By using their CPA program they have created a framework that identifies who will address an issue.

Similarly, they use customer focus groups as part of their corrective and preventive action process to help them focus on customer needs. The results of these group meetings are then incorporated into executive summaries to help them resolve issues. This program allows them to initiate process changes within their own group or across the company. Most important, their corrective and preventive action program focuses on processes rather than on individuals. This has allowed them to avoid emphasizing that an individual has made an error or finding someone to blame for a problem. ISO registration and the corrective and preventive action program have created a healthy collaborative focus allowing the management team to work together to solve systems and process problems, to satisfy customer needs, and to seek opportunities for improvements in their processes. In addition to being a great morale boost and sense of common achievement, ISO caused managers to recognize that even when they are successfully managing their own departments, they need to understand how hand-offs to other divisions within the company affect the satisfaction of the ultimate customer.

19

~❧ ❧~

Section 4.15, Handling, Storage, Packaging, Preservation, and Delivery

THE KEY QUESTIONS

Section 4.15, Handling, Storage, Packaging, Preservation, and Delivery (HSPPD), asks:

1. Can we carefully handle, package, store, preserve, and deliver physical components of our service so they reach our customer undamaged?
2. Can we protect our people while they handle, package, store, preserve, and deliver physical components of our service?

INTERPRETING THE STANDARD

This section of the standard addresses routine issues related to protecting product from damage or deterioration while it is in the hands of the ISO 9000-registered company. Each of the five subsections addresses one area and focuses on the notion of protecting the product. The 1994 version strengthened the section by adding the requirement for preservation; that is, protecting the product from damage and deterioration. Although the section does not refer specifically to employees or address the need to protect employees who handle the product, auditors and companies are aware that employee safety concerns are part of the overall intent of the standard. In addition, although the standard seems to imply that storage activities are limited to warehouses or specific storage areas, many companies consider product and parts in process waiting for the next step to be in storage even though they are on the production line. In any case, just as it is necessary to always know the current inspection status of all products, as is required by Section 4.12, it is always necessary to protect the product when it is under the control of the company.

The section calls for procedures—plural—to address these HSPPD issues. That may be interpreted either as a separate procedure for each subclause or as some combination of procedures, as long as each of the activities is adequately addressed and controlled. In addition to a procedure or procedures, this section requires the company to:

- Protect the product—and the persons who handle the product—during any handling or moving activities
- Provide designated stock rooms—or safe areas—for finished or in-process product
- Control methods to issue product into and to remove product from storage areas
- Conduct a routine inventory to assess the condition of product in storage
- Establish methods and use of materials for packing product to protect it during shipment
- Establish methods to preserve and segregate product as appropriate to protect it
- Make arrangements for safe shipment or, when contractually specified, until delivery

This section of the standard is oriented around physical products, and its root intention is to protect and preserve the product and subcomponents of the product from damage and/or deterioration while under the control of the ISO company.

Service Perspectives on HSPPD

This is another section that reflects the original manufacturing mentality of the standard's authors. Other than transshippers or distribution centers whose service is to handle products, service organizations that do not specifically handle products would not apply this section of the standard, or would use some other section of the standard to cover related activities. For example, some service companies might handle, transfer, or forward customer information; however, that activity is probably better controlled under Section 4.16, Control of Quality Records. An airline would handle baggage and passengers, but those activities could be addressed under Section 4.9, Process Control. A medical doctor may actually handle a patient, but again that would be part of process control rather than Section 4.15 because the patient is not the product or service—the service provided is the medical care the patient receives from the doctor. Sometimes service providers use parts, tools, or supplies in the process of delivering their service. However, protection of these items can be easily addressed under another section of the standard, or as a subsection of a procedure or work instruction, rather than calling them out separately in a procedure on HSPPD. It might be possible to consider parts and supplies such as office supplies, or spare bulbs, as being in storage and that this section might apply to these kinds of activities. But generally—except for repair parts and preventive maintenance supplies—registrar auditors do not tend to define these items as items in storage.

PRACTICAL EXAMPLES

- To establish *"appropriate methods for authorizing receipt to and dispatch from"* storage, a self-storage facility may require customers to sign in when entering the premises.
- To *"apply appropriate methods for preservation,"* a wholesale distributor may provide climate-controlled storage facilities.
- To *"arrange for the protection of the quality of product,"* a city water-treatment facility may upgrade underground water pipes in an older neighborhood.

COMPLYING WITH SECTION 4.15 IN SERVICE ORGANIZATIONS

Determine if HSPPD Is Part of Your Activity

As part of your process flowcharting and procedure development process, determine if HSPPD is really part of your service, or whether it is possible to cover these activities under another relevant section of the standard.

Protect Products and People

Although the standard does not specifically address protecting employees during handling activities, all companies should be aware that employee safety is implicit within this section. In addition, other sections in the standard—for example, Section 4.9b— refers to a "suitable working environment," and Section 4.9c refers to "reference standards/codes." These include OSHA, EPA, and other safety-related regulatory codes.

Case Study in Handling, Storage, Packaging, Preservation, and Delivery

The United Parcel Service (UPS) Package Lab designs, tests, and provides packaging for anything manufacturers and shippers need to transport, from such high-technology shipments as computers and electronic gear, to documents. The lab is co-located with the 6,000-person UPS Chicago Area Consolidation Hub (CACH), the state-of-the-art, automated sorting facility through which UPS moves 1.2 million packages each day. The UPS CACH is the primary ground transport hub in their national hub-and-spoke system. Other operating centers serve as regional hubs. UPS' primary US air transport hub is in Louisville, KY, and is augmented by 5 regional air hubs and 7 gateways around the world. Worldwide, 331,000 UPS employees handle 12 million parcels and documents every day.

The Package Lab operates under UPS Professional Services, Inc., which is chartered to provide consulting solutions and professional services for its clients, and is one of several UPS organizations separately registered to ISO. The lab sought and received ISO 9001 registration in 1995. According to Dennis Amato, the Package Lab Manager, UPS has always considered itself a high-quality organization. As early as 1907, their slogan was "The Best Service at the Lowest Rates." UPS views ISO registration as one way to demonstrate to customers and the public their use of quality principles to guide their business. In addition to ISO, the Package Lab also uses a Quality Improvement Process to measure their business from their clients' point of view, to improve processes and customer satisfaction, and to reduce claims. The UPS Customer Satisfaction Index (CSI) is a further measure of their service performance.

The lab provides packaging solutions to clients through testing and design of various packing and materials. Chad Thompson, UPS Corporate Packaging Engineer, is one of three consultants who works with national account clients to ensure that the packaging protects their products so that they arrive undamaged. In addition to the external package, the lab also evaluates packing materials used inside the package. The lab provides a wide range of testing, including vibration, shock, and compression tests for packages and packing materials. The test package or materials are inspected and flow through a control and inspection process as they are tested. Usually, the tests include a 60-minute vibration test, along with a 10-point, free-fall drop sequence.

As part of UPS' environmental protection initiatives, the Package Lab also helps clients explore environmentally-sound alternatives to minimize packaging, thereby reducing waste while ensuring the safest and most cost-effective methods of shipping. UPS has defined a series of steps to either dispose of the materials or deliver them back to the client after testing is complete.

As required by ISO, all of the lab's handling, storage, packaging, preservation, and delivery steps are described in procedures and work instructions. Importantly, however, these procedures and work instructions have been integrated into their process control documentation rather than being established as separate documents under this section. Their quality manual refers readers to the process control section for documentation covering HSPPD.

LESSONS LEARNED

Like many companies and organizations, the UPS Package Lab thought they had a good quality foundation in place, and they decided to use their ISO registration as a complement to their existing programs. The lab reports one of the best outcomes of ISO is a stronger corrective and preventive action program that ensures that refinements and improvements become routine practice and that corrected deficiencies do not reoccur. Additionally, ISO helped the lab evaluate and fine-tune their existing programs by defining how they would interpret the ISO standard and other quality initiatives and then establishing who would be responsible for these interpretations. That has allowed the lab to integrate several quality initiatives and avoid lengthy discussions to resolve issues.

Most important, the lab has done two things well. They have integrated their ISO program into existing quality initiatives and integrated the standard requirements into their procedures and work instructions, rather than trying to integrate their procedures and work instructions into a structure based on the requirements of the ISO standard. By satisfying the HSPPD requirements within their process control activities, the lab has wisely met the *intent* of the standard without being limited to a structure organized rigidly around the standard. In short, the lab has taken advantage of the generic requirements in the standard to fit their business needs and help them achieve their customer goals.

20

꿏 ꙮ

Section 4.16,
Control of Quality Records

Section 4.16, Control of Quality Records, asks:

1. Do we know which records will demonstrate the successful completion of our service?
2. Are our records legible and useful?
3. Do we provide safe storage, and can we retrieve records when we need them?

INTERPRETING THE STANDARD

A basic tenet of ISO 9000 is to "Say What You Do, and Do What You Say." Records provide the objective "do what you say" evidence that an activity took place. In ISO parlance, *objective evidence* is a verifiable statement of fact or a written record of an activity. Because records and objective evidence are fundamental to the basic philosophy of ISO, this section of the standard is particularly important for companies seeking registration. Records control, which includes control of records from subcontractors, is one of the areas registrars will examine most closely.

The standard makes reference to *quality records*. This terminology may lead some companies astray. All records are quality records because they are evidence of activities and tasks. Like the requirement for process documentation, the requirement to keep quality records frequently evokes fears of complexity and difficulties in management. Just as with process documentation, however, this requirement does not need to be overwhelming and offers companies some practical advantages. Importantly, the standard does not require an elaborate system, nor is it necessary to handle every record with the same level of control. Auditors will be concerned that records are available and legible, and they will be concerned records are kept in appropriate areas as reflected in the company's quality plan. It remains the company's responsibility to determine exactly which records are involved and how they will be managed.

The standard identifies a minimum of 18 categories or kinds of records that must be maintained. Those requirements are specified in each section by inclusion of the parenthetical statement "(See 4.16)," which refers back to this section. Just as Section 4.5, Document and Data Control, does not establish specific requirements for the documents themselves, but rather requires identifying how documents will be controlled, Section 4.16, Control of Quality Records, does not tell the company specifically which records it must keep. The requirements for the types of records that must be maintained are established within the relevant sections of the standard. Rather, Section 4.16 sets forth how a company must approach keeping their records. Essentially, the company must have a system that addresses eight basic records-keeping tasks—identifying, collecting, indexing, accessing, filing, storing, maintaining, and disposing of records.

Once the basic eight records-keeping and handling requirements are met and a procedure covering these processes is in place, the standard establishes four basic requirements for all records. They are as follows:

- Records must be legible
- Records must be protected in a suitable environment, particularly while in storage
- Records must be readily retrievable and available when needed
- Records retention times must be established and adhered to

Records from subcontractors or vendors also are part of the records-keeping program, and when required by contract, records must be available for customers' review for a specified period of time. Also, a note in the standard advises companies that they are welcome to use electronic media or computer databases as a way to maintain records.

SERVICE PERSPECTIVES ON CONTROL OF QUALITY RECORDS

There is no appreciable difference between the needs of manufacturing companies and service organizations for records-keeping. Both kinds of companies must maintain—at a minimum—the 18 categories of records required by the standard. Records serve several purposes for both types of organizations. Most importantly, as the standard says, they "demonstrate conformance to specified requirements and the effective operation of the quality system." They help an organization demonstrate that it continues to monitor and improve its processes and outcomes to meet customer needs.

The real challenge for any company approaching its records-keeping program is to decide which records are needed, how long they must be maintained, how they will be handled, and when and how they will be disposed of. Of these decisions, probably the most difficult decision is trying to make sure the company is disposing of appropriately unneeded records. Unfortunately, many folks believe they must have an individual "copy for my files" or they must keep records into perpetuity. Neither of these beliefs is correct. Legal requirements establish the periods of time some records, such as tax reports or human resources files, must be maintained. As part of its overall responsibility, management must assess risks and determine to what extent its operations can be protected by maintaining certain kinds of records. In any case, the ISO registration project provides a service company with a good opportunity to do a thorough housecleaning and dispose of unneeded records. It also is an opportunity to determine which records no longer must be kept. That is, the ISO program can help eliminate the need to maintain some records in the first place.

Once the company determines which records it needs and how long various categories of records will be maintained, it is then necessary to decide how the records will be physically handled. The eight verbs—identify, collect, index, access, file, store, maintain, and dispose of—provide the foundation for any organized method of handling records. ISO registrars do not judge the records-keeping system itself. They are interested in knowing whether your service company's records-keeping system meets your needs and works for you. Once that question, along with the other *shalls* specified in this section of the standard, is addressed you are at liberty to use any method that suits your needs.

PRACTICAL EXAMPLES

- In order to arrange for the *"identification, collection, indexing, access, filing, storage, maintenance, and disposition of quality records,"* a hospital may use entirely paperless operations, relying instead on multiple terminals, including bedside terminals, for entry of patient records.
- To maintain records *"to demonstrate conformance to specified requirements,"* a long-distance trucker may maintain a driving log to demonstrate compliance with company and regulatory requirements for taking adequate rest periods.
- To specify *"retention times of quality records,"* a multinational mergers and acquisitions firm may establish a master list of records and their retention times.

COMPLYING WITH SECTION 4.16 IN SERVICE ORGANIZATIONS

Clean House

Find out which records are being maintained, who is maintaining these records, and in what format or location they are being maintained. Then determine a rationale for which records should be continued and which can be eliminated. Use the ISO registration project as an opportunity to ruthlessly clean house of unneeded records.

Adopt an Efficient System

There are several good books on records-keeping systems available and there is an organization of professional records administrators. You should spend sufficient time to think about what kind of system you need and particularly how you can have a simple system that will work well to satisfy your needs.

Go Electronic When Possible

ISO allows your service organization to use electronic media for both documentation and records-keeping activities. This requires an investment in hardware, software, and learning time to move to an electronic records-keeping system. The investment, however, usually is easily recouped within a short period in increased efficiency, reduction in expense for paper and physical records storage, and heightened record useability.

CONTROL OF QUALITY RECORDS IN THE CASE STUDIES

Records-keeping may appear on the surface as a trivial, mechanical matter appropriately delegated to clerks. However, because ISO 9000 is based on the concept "Say What You Do and Do What You Say," a good records-keeping system is essential to a successful ISO program. Records are the objective evidence that the quality system is meeting the needs of the company and its customers. The standard's requirements are straightforward, and as long as they and the eight verbs describing requirements are met, any records-keeping system that works well for the company is satisfactory. Whatever the system, salvation is in the details.

Interviews for this book's case studies revealed several general themes in how companies manage records-keeping.

- Records come in many formats, from simple memoranda to forms to complex legal documents. Records such as computer printouts and customer-supplied records, such as shipping documents and contracts, are also part of the records-keeping files and fall under the requirements of the ISO standard.
- The ISO registration process is a wonderful opportunity to clean house. Many companies and individuals either ignore or hoard records. Although many of us tend to identify critical records, such as legal, human resources, and tax records, and do a good job handling those types of records for which a legal requirement is established, we may ignore other kinds of records, such as memoranda and meeting minutes, and rely on individuals to establish and use whatever kind of system seems reasonable. Unfortunately, records may be perceived as a low priority by some individuals, leading to lost, damaged,

or inconsistently maintained records. By establishing a simple, consistent method throughout the organization, these problems can be eliminated, along with unneeded and redundant records.

- Electronic or computer records-keeping methods are prevalent in many service organizations—as well as manufacturing companies—and help eliminate many problems formerly associated with records-keeping.

LESSONS LEARNED

The most significant difficulty reported by several companies was differentiating between records and documents, since the terms frequently are used interchangeably. The requirements in the ISO standard, however, are different for records than for documents. A *document* is something that describes an activity or tells individuals how to perform a task. Work instructions and procedures are documents. They may be used as part of an ongoing process over time. *Records* chronicle a specific event. They are used one time.

Confusion sometimes occurs over forms and/or plans. A blank form is a document and its design and control are covered under the requirements of Section 4.5, Document and Data Control. Once the form is used or filled in, that particular form—be it a piece of paper or an electronic screen—becomes a record and falls under the requirements of Section 4.16, Control of Quality Records. Similarly, a plan or schedule is a document. However, once it is used or enacted, it becomes a record.

The second key problem reported by companies is trying to differentiate between records and quality records. This is a terminology misinterpretation. There is no difference. All records are quality records and must be controlled under the requirements of this section of the standard.

21

Section 4.17, Internal Quality Audits

THE KEY QUESTIONS

Section 4.17, Internal Quality Audits, asks:

1. Are we effectively using an ongoing self-assessment process that helps us maintain and improve our work processes?
2. Are we able to demonstrate that we "Say What We Do and Do What We Say"?
3. Is there a process in place to conduct systems and compliance assessments to demonstrate that an effective ISO 9000 program is helping our company reach its strategic goals?

INTERPRETING THE STANDARD

The third step in the Plan, Do, Check, Act of the Shewhart Cycle—Check—is represented by this section of the ISO 9000 standard. *Internal quality audits,* or *first-party audits,* are self-assessments that help companies: first, ensure that documentation is adequate to meet the standard requirements, which is a *systems audit;* and, second, to make sure the company follows its plans and procedures, that is, a *compliance audit*. Section 4.2.2a, Quality System Procedures, requires companies to establish documented procedures to meet their needs—the system—and Section 4.2.2b requires companies to follow their established documented processes—compliance.

Section 4.17 requires both a systems and a compliance audit.

Essentially, the standard requires the company to do a self-assessment to make sure its quality assurance process is working well. The language of the standard says "to verify whether quality activities and related results comply with planned arrangements and to determine the effectiveness of the quality system."

In addition to a procedure that describes the process as well as the records of the audits, the standard stipulates several additional requirements. They are as follows:

- Audits must focus on activities and processes most important to the company
- Persons directly responsible for an area may not audit their own functions/areas
- Line supervision responsible for the audited area must be informed of the audit results and take timely action to correct deficiencies
- Follow-up audits must be conducted to make sure corrective actions are implemented and effective

Interestingly enough, there also is a requirement that the company have individuals who are trained to serve as internal auditors. This requirement, however, is not contained in Section 4.17. It is found in Section 4.1.2.2, Resources. It says, "The supplier shall . . . provide adequate resources, including . . . trained personnel . . . for . . . verification activities including internal quality audits." By identifying the need for trained internal auditors as part of the general requirements early in the standard, the writers have emphasized its importance. Typically two- to three-day internal audit training programs teach employees how to interpret the ISO standard, how to plan and conduct audits, and how to report audit results.

SERVICE PERSPECTIVES ON INTERNAL QUALITY AUDITS

There really is little difference between a good internal quality audit program for a manufacturing company and one for a service company. Regardless of the type of organization, an effective internal audit program will help identify areas of concern and opportunities for improvement. Done well, the program can be a wonderful, cost-effective tool to help management and employees find more effective and efficient ways to deliver its services. It is very important to emphasize that the internal audit program should be used to assess the quality management systems and should not be used to look at individual or group performances. If there is a personnel or discipline problem, those issues should be handled through routine human resources processes, not the ISO program. Also, it is important for everyone to recognize that the outcomes and findings from the audit program provide the company with opportunities to find more effective and efficient processes and to adopt best practices to accomplish activities. The company's internal audit program, along with Management Review (Section 4.1.3) and Corrective and Preventive Action (Section 4.14) are the three cornerstones to a solid ISO quality management program.

In addition to a procedure to drive your service company's internal audit program, you will need an annual audit schedule in order to ensure that all areas and functions within your organization are audited against the relevant sections of the standard at least once per year. The internal audit program should include a look at all company procedures, plans, and work instructions, too. Your audit program should include routine looks at codes and standards, such as safety and environmental, federal, state, and local regulations, that the company must follow. There is a requirement in this section that the scheduled audits be based on the "status and importance of the activity to be audited." That means routine processes and those that are working well do not need frequent audits. However, changes to processes, new machines, equipment, markets, employee turnover in an area, customer complaints, trends or statistics that indicate problems, or potential problem areas should all be considered for more frequent audits.

You will need trained internal auditors. The typical internal auditor training program is two or three days during which participants learn how to interpret and apply the requirements of the standard, and how to organize an audit, conduct interviews, gather objective evidence, report findings, and prepare an audit report. A good internal audit program will draw auditors from all areas or functions within the company and from all levels within the hierarchy. It is a good idea to ask for volunteers and to ask selected individuals to volunteer. The more people who are involved from the broadest base possible will help ensure that everyone takes ownership of the program. These internal auditors can also serve a dual role because they will serve as ambassadors for the ISO program and are able to take ideas back to their functions or groups, help them become prepared for future audits, and to improve their own area's compliance to the standard.

Finally, a good internal audit program will separate the internal audit process from the corrective and preventive action program. Auditors should audit and line management should fix problems. A good internal audit program also will limit the scope of its activities to the absolute minimum to be effective. The ISO 10011, Guidelines for Auditing Quality Systems, particularly cautions companies to ensure that line management—the people who actually perform the activities—take responsibility for corrective actions rather than transferring that responsibility to the audit group. It states, "Quality audits should not result in a transfer of the responsibility to achieve quality from operating staff to the auditing organization." The guideline also cautions companies to avoid creating a complex, resource-intensive auditing program that becomes a fiefdom unto itself. It says, "Quality audits should not lead to an increase in the scope of quality functions over and above those necessary to meet quality objectives." Or, more simply, keep the program as simple as possible to do a good job.

PRACTICAL EXAMPLES

- To *"verify whether quality activities and related results comply with planned arrangements and to determine the effectiveness of the quality system,"* a software development firm may schedule and conduct monthly miniaudits of their entire ISO 9001 management system so at the end of each year, they have audited each area at least one time.
- To schedule audits *"on the basis of the status and importance of the activity to be audited,"* an airport management group may conduct quarterly operational audits of their emergency response teams, which they perceive to be very important.
- To conduct follow-up activities to *"verify and record the implementation and effectiveness of the corrective action taken,"* a personnel department manager may routinely schedule quarterly

follow-up assessments of closed nonconformances for his department.

COMPLYING WITH SECTION 4.17 IN SERVICE ORGANIZATIONS

Train a Cadre of Auditors

Ask for volunteers and select representatives from all areas within the company and from all levels within the hierarchy to serve as internal auditors. As a rule-of-thumb, select and train about 15 internal auditors or about 10 percent of the employees, whichever is lower—very small companies may elect to have one or two trained internal auditors and rely on outside help to supplement their program. Having a cadre of trained internal auditors will reduce the burden on any one or small group of individuals to conduct all of the audits. With this many auditors, each individual could be limited to three or four days per year in service as an auditor. Also, you will probably have some turnover, and some individuals will simply decide they do not want to serve.

Stress the Positive Outcomes

Too frequently both employees and the internal auditors perceive their role as company enforcer, to seek out and punish the guilty. This is not true. Good internal auditors are sensitive to the potential employee perception that his or her job performance is being scrutinized and the individual employee is open to blame for nonconformances. A good internal audit program will emphasize two concepts—first, audits look at systems, not people, and second, audits are opportunities for improvement. Employees and auditors both need to emphasize the positive outcomes of the internal audit program.

Separate Audits from Corrective and Preventive Action

Your auditors' job is to conduct systems and compliance audits. Do not allow your auditors to turn into consultants or to try to help line supervisors fix problems. This is strictly a political issue. It is difficult enough to overcome employees' belief that the audit program is designed to point out their shortcomings. Employees—auditees—will quickly become resentful of individuals who not only identify the problems but then try to tell them how to do their jobs.

Use ISO 10011, Guidelines for Auditing Quality Systems

This ISO guideline is an excellent and practical basis around which you can organize your internal audit program. The guideline is written to help all kinds of companies organize any kind of audit, and even registrars use it to structure how they conduct audits. There is some very sound advice in the guideline, particularly the idea that line management is responsible for fixing problems, not the auditors. The guideline is also pragmatic when it cautions companies not to create a major undertaking and multiple audits, and suggests the audit program should be limited to the absolute minimum effort needed to be successful.

CASE STUDY IN INTERNAL QUALITY AUDITS

The Dow Chemical Company has about 43,000 employees worldwide. The Dow Customer Service Center is one of many units that is separately registered to ISO 9002. There are about 150 employees at the center, of which 12 are managers, 15 are administrators, and 120 are account representatives. Their primary tasks are to process customer inquiries, orders, and adjustments and to serve as a central order processing service support center for the 100 or so Dow Company manufacturing operations.

Starting in 1988, the Customer Service Center undertook three major concurrent projects. They centralized the activities of six regional offices and 27 sales offices into one main office, they adopted a new enterprise-database computer system, and they began the process of seeking ISO 9000 registration. The three projects were mutually supporting, and the synergy from the first two contributed to their registration effort. Early in the project, they found the sales offices and regional offices did not have a consistent, standardized, documented way to perform their tasks. They also found the new computer system provided an opportunity to design a new way to efficiently perform tasks. Working to consolidate the offices and bring the new computer system on-line, they involved everyone in the project and divided into teams to identify the components of their individual and collective activities and tasks. The new computer system in particular helped focus on the differences among their current practices and to seek best practices using the new database. Their ISO internal audit program provided the engine that helped document work processes to support the new systems as they were implemented.

Of the 150 individuals at the center, 12 are trained Customer Service internal auditors. Frequently, they also borrow someone from another Dow business unit or someone from a local outside company, and they have called on a former employee to help them part-time with their program. One of their members is a certified lead assessor; all have been trained as internal auditors. Their annual audit schedule is established to ensure that they look at each section and every process at least once per year. Because of the nature of their business, they look at document control several times each year and they look at contract review—because it is the most important part of their activities—every time they audit. The Customer Service Center also typically schedules some time during each audit for follow-up activities so the auditors can review closed corrective and preventive action reports from previous audit findings.

As a general rule, they conduct monthly Customer Service Audits. The Customer Service Quality Manager and Management Representative is their audit coordinator and is responsible for scheduling auditors and auditees, as well as logistics for each audit. The auditors are divided into two teams of five or six people, and each team works every other month. Each auditor prepares for interviews with three or four people, which takes about 5 hours in a typical audit day. Therefore, each individual devotes five or six days per year to the internal audit program.

Twice each year, the entire team comes together for a joint meeting to review their internal audit program. The team shares experiences, looking for things they have learned and identifying changes in the organization or its practices they may want to look at more closely. The team adjusts their annual schedule accordingly. These semiannual internal auditor meetings serve as the foundation to prepare a report that becomes part of the ISO 9000 management review process required in Section 4.1.3.

LESSONS LEARNED

Undertaking three significant concurrent projects may have seemed a monumental task. However, the folks at Dow Service

Center discovered that by involving everyone in the process, they were able to find synergy among the projects, that their ISO registration process helped them as they established documentation and methods to design and bring on-line their new computer system and to integrate their previously separate offices. It was a large adjustment for many individuals to live within such a system, and at first people were nervous because they incorrectly perceived the internal audit program as a measure of their individual performances, rather than as a review of the work systems. One of the things the Customer Service Center has continued to emphasize is that audits are not a measure of the individuals' ability to do their jobs. Rather it is a look at the work processes and systems to make sure the systems are effective and efficient.

Their new computer system has been especially helpful in providing data on order entry errors and customer satisfaction results. The Customer Service Center has been able to use the data to improve their work processes. Their organizational restructuring has brought all individuals performing this function under one roof and allowed them to figure out and adopt best practices to do their work. Their internal audit process has given them insight into new ideas and ways to improve their service. And their semiannual auditor meetings have helped them capture the organizational knowledge generated from their internal audit program.

22

⮚ ⮘

Section 4.18, Training

THE KEY QUESTIONS

Section 4.18, Training, asks:

1. Do we know what training and experience our people need to do their jobs successfully?
2. Do we provide the training or ensure that our people have the experience they need?

INTERPRETING THE STANDARD

The notion that companies need trained employees appears in several places in the ISO 9000 standard. For example, Section 4.1.2.2, Resources, identifies the need for trained and experienced personnel as one measure of adequate resources. Section 4.2.2, Quality System Procedures, refers to the "skills and training needed by personnel involved in carrying out the activity." Section 4.4.2, Design and Development Planning, requires design work be carried out by "qualified personnel." Also, Section 4.9, Process Control, makes reference to "qualified operators." Finally, Section 4.18, Training, requires the company to determine what training and experience personnel need to do their jobs and to provide that training to them. In addition to a procedure, the section on training requires the company to maintain training records for personnel.

There are two confusing statements in this section. The first wording refers to "personnel performing activities affecting quality." That phrase is misleading because every individual and every activity at some level affects quality. If the individual or the tasks and activities performed do not contribute to the company's goals and objectives, they probably are nonvalue-added wastes of resources and should be eliminated. The second statement refers to "personnel performing specific assigned tasks." Again, every position—regardless of where it is in the organizational hierarchy—should have a job or tasks description, and the individuals working in those positions should be performing those tasks. The language in the standard may lead some practitioners astray in an effort to exclude some persons and tasks as not relating to quality. For example, they may try to exclude staff and support personnel. These attempts are bound to result in confusion and frustration as practitioners try to decide who should and who should not be included in the definition. In addition, such an approach will open them to potential questions from their registrar as they attempt to explain and justify their decisions. It is much easier and more simple to include everyone in the company within the scope of the training procedure. Practitioners should identify every core task and develop reasonable education and training requirements as needed for each individual in the company.

SERVICE PERSPECTIVES ON TRAINING

Fundamentally, there is little difference between the need for training for manufacturing and for service personnel. In both arenas, employees must have the required skills and knowledge to successfully carry out their assigned tasks. There are obvious differences in the subject matter content needed across various industries and within different settings. Manufacturing employees may need more specific skills-based training, whereas service employees may need more general skills. But there are probably more common skills and knowledge across both groups than there are differences. Both service and manufacturing employees need such skills and knowledge as use of quality tools, team behaviors, and written and oral communication skills. In the end, all employees must know their jobs and must either receive the training or the company must hire personnel who have the requisite skills and knowledge.

Service personnel who directly deal with customers may need

specific training to help them learn how to interact one-on-one with customers, how to diagnose situations, and how to respond appropriately to customer needs. Therefore, they will need good interpersonal skills as well as both written and oral communication skills. It is probably more cost-effective to select employees with an appropriate level of these basic skills rather than attempting to train the skills for new employees. Additionally, service employees will need to know the technical or subject matter content of their jobs and how to perform their assigned tasks. These skills can be taught and should be part of both initial and ongoing—or professional enhancement—training conducted by the company.

PRACTICAL EXAMPLES

- To identify *"training needs and provide for the training of all personnel,"* a city law enforcement department may provide emergency medical technician training to its peace/public service officers.
- To ensure *"personnel performing specific assigned tasks shall be qualified,"* a union may provide training and certification for its member welders.
- To maintain *"appropriate records of training,"* a regional bank may maintain a database of the training each of their employees has successfully completed.

COMPLYING WITH SECTION 4.18 IN SERVICE ORGANIZATIONS

Matrix Skills Needed to Jobs

Brainstorm a list of core skills and knowledge for each job position in your organization. Keep the list simple and general. Develop a one-page matrix of jobs—not positions or individuals assigned to jobs—to skills and knowledge needed. It may be possible to have several individuals or positions doing the same job. Include this matrix as an appendix to your procedure on training. You can then also develop a more detailed checklist of skills and training to include in each individual's training record. The checklist can serve as a planning device to help employees map their future training, and it can also serve as a record of the training completed.

Determine Training Strategies

Use the most efficient opportunity to train personnel. It is not necessary to rely strictly on classic classroom sessions. On-the-job training (OJT) is an excellent way to make sure individuals are able to perform their tasks. Employees can observe an experienced individual and also work under the supervision of an experienced person to learn a task. Brief training sessions can also be included as part of other routine meetings, such as safety, staff, or sales meetings. Attendance at conferences and professional meetings should also be considered as part of the training program.

Capture Training Records

Attendance sheets capture classroom training results. Minutes of meetings—which note attendees—can be used to capture records when training activities are conducted in this format. If check sheets or forms are used to perform tasks, use those as a way to capture OJT records. For example, have the supervisor observe an employee complete a task using a work instruction or check sheet. Have the supervisor sign and date the work instruction as a record the individual has mastered the task. When employees attend professional meetings or conferences, have them write a short—two-sentence— report about the information learned at the meeting as part of their reimbursement expense report and use that as a training record. Tying the report to their expense reimbursement is an excellent motivator for employees to submit the record.

CASE STUDY IN TRAINING

Mary Kay Hopkins, Inc. (REALTORS), lists and sells residential real estate and provides relocation services and mortgage origination services for individuals and companies in Lake Charles and Calcasieu Parish, Louisiana. Their 160,000 market population area economy is based primarily on petrochemical industries, aircraft manufacturing, and the gaming/tourist industry. Mary Kay Hopkins (CRB), a licensed broker, is president of the company, which has served the area for more than 20 years. The company consists of four full- and two part-time administrative assistants and 15 real estate agents. The closing coordinator's specialized tasks include all activities from the time a property first sells through closing. The relocation coordinator supervises relocation activities. These activities include tracking referral activity, listing, and managing corporate properties. The administrative coordinator performs general, routine tasks, including receptionist activities. She also coordinates the Mary Kay Hopkins weekly TV show.

An inventory coordinator maintains their multilist (MLS) to track property listing, property status changes, sales and closing of properties, and ensures that the MLS books are updated. The 15 sales agents are independent contractors—selected and qualified under the requirements of Section 4.6, Purchasing—and are responsible to list and sell properties for the company. As part of the purchasing process, the company established a hiring standard, as well as a standard of practices their agents are expected to follow.

To qualify to be hired at Mary Kay Hopkins, Inc., an agent must have completed a Louisiana state-accredited real estate course, have two years experience as a real estate agent, and/or undergo the Mary Kay Hopkins training program. To obtain a license to list and sell real estate in the state of Louisiana, agents must accomplish certain state-mandated training requirements. In addition to the 90-hour accredited training program and successful completion of a two-part exam covering both state and national regulations, Louisiana real estate agents must complete 8 hours per year of continuing training offered by the Louisiana Realtors Association, real estate schools or local colleges, or the state real estate commission. The requirements vary from state to state; however, in most states, the requirements are relatively similar and provide a foundation or base knowledge.

When Mary Kay Hopkins began to address the training requirements in Section 4.18 as part of their journey to ISO registration, they realized they had been doing a lot of good training beyond the state-mandated requirements, and they had many success stories they could attribute to their competent and capable agents. However, they did not have an organized training program, and most of the training was scheduled on a hit-or-miss basis. Frequently, despite their good intentions and best efforts, they were not maximizing their return on the resources spent on training, because they were not sufficiently well organized to ensure that the training was completed, nor were they able to capture the records of the training to ensure that everyone had completed the necessary work. ISO registration provided an opportunity to bring their program into focus and to structure much of they were doing.

First, Mary Kay, as president of the company, started by creating a training-requirements matrix listing each position across the top and down the left-hand column the needed skills and knowledge, including software and office skills, telephone skills, report writing, third-party relocation practices and requirements, various mortgage computations, legal requirements, and closing forms and practices, among others. Once she identified all of the activities, skills, and knowledge an agent would need to be well trained and successful, it was a simple matter to place Xs in the matrix to indicate which positions needed which skills and knowledge. With this matrix of needs and requirements in hand, it was then possible to design and implement the company's training program and write their training procedure.

The standards of practice by which administrative staff and sales agents must abide was developed by Mary Kay as a joint effort with all of the staff. Together they defined the training program in the company's job descriptions and procedures. The procedures serve a dual function in that they describe the responsibilities and authorities as required in Section 4.1.2.1, Responsibility and Authority, and they serve as a checklist of topics to describe the skills and knowledge employees need to successfully perform their jobs.

In order to ensure that both administrative staff and sales agents are knowledgeable and skilled to meet the standards of practice and performance, Mary Kay and her staff have developed a fairly extensive training program for all members of the company. They use several strategies to conduct the training, both formal classroom as well as OJT and group meetings. They set up training sessions with various invited expert guest presenters, including a property appraiser, an attorney, and a bank loan officer, among others. Their own experienced sales personnel present some of the sessions, also. Additionally, new employees attend listing and sales presentations, mortgage origination, and final closings meetings with another agent, and are assigned to observe a variety of other related tasks with an agent or staff member. They also conduct market analyses with another agent and practice on their own. All of this is in addition to the basic state-required program. In addition to 150 hours of prework, self-study, and field work, each Mary Kay employee spends about 160 hours in the company-sponsored basic training program.

Agent and staff training does not stop once the basic program is completed. The entire staff conducts routine ongoing short training sessions as part of routine sales and staff meetings. For example, they will review various parts of closing procedures and forms over a four- or five-week period as part of the weekly sales meeting, which serves as refresher training for everyone, and allows everyone to share experiences and lessons learned. Also, when there are changes to procedures or forms, either as a result of an external source or something within the staff's own operation, or new information to learn, such as changes to brokerage law, the company devotes part of their weekly sales meeting to this type of training. As part of their ongoing training the staff also conducts one-on-one training sessions on an as-needed basis for agents or staff who need to refresh or enhance skills, particularly in areas such as forms, applications, or software requirements.

The basic sales training program is conducted at least every two years and is revised every time it is conducted. As Mary Kay presents the training, she has found gaps or information that needed to be added. This has caused Mary Kay to amend and update both the matrix of required training, as well as the company's procedures and job descriptions. Mary Kay thinks their ISO training program is significantly better than the way they provided training in the past. However, even now, after having gone through their recertification audit and having begun their second year as an ISO 9002 company, they still believe they can improve their program. As Mary Kay says, "We are not at the 'really proud of it' stage yet, but we are getting there."

LESSONS LEARNED

Mary Kay Hopkins,Inc. learned about ISO through the local American Society of Quality/Lake Charles Chapter, which is very active in its community. The company had been working on applying various total quality tools and techniques when the chapter hosted an informational meeting about ISO 9000. Mary Kay immediately saw ISO as a way to provide a basic foundation for all of the quality initiatives her company had been trying to implement. She knew that TQM could help her company do their work better, but they were struggling to get over some hurdles simply because they did not have a solid, overarching foundation on which to build their quality program.

Mary Kay also thought the company had a good training program and routinely had earned a 98 percent customer satisfaction ratings as evidence that their agents are competent and capable. On its surface, it would have appeared that a more structured program and additional training was not really necessary. However, that surface assumption has been proven wrong. The company has continued to maintain its excellent customer ratings; however, the difference has been readily evident in the company's increased efficiency and in the agents' greater self-confidence. Mary Kay and her staff have found that their ISO-documented systems and structured records-keeping methods have freed everyone to focus on providing excellent service to their customers. The agents and staff are more self-confident and rely less on Mary Kay, and she is more confident of the capabilities of her agents and staff. Thanks in part to their training program, Mary Kay now spends less time on routine administrative work or working with individual agents, and is able to devote more time to the community and to individual customers.

23

`-ᴈ ʀ-`

Section 4.19, Servicing

THE KEY QUESTION

Section 4.19, Servicing, asks:

1. If we supply service under a servicing contract, do we know what processes we need and whether those processes are effective and efficient?

INTERPRETING THE STANDARD

Servicing is not service. Service is an activity or series of activities that provide value to customers. ISO categorizes service as a product. Servicing, on the other hand, includes two broad categories of activities. The first is postwarranty repairs—after the warranty expires—to a product by the producer of the product. Typically, people buy postwarranty repair contracts on automobiles, computers, refrigerators, and other appliances. The other category of service contract is a maintenance and repair contract sold by a company that did not originally produce the product. For example, a photocopier retailer may offer a servicing contract to a lessee. The contract specifies that the retailer will clean and provide toner and other supplies on a routine basis, as well as provide repair services—usually within a guaranteed time frame.

If the company provides servicing as part of its activities, it must have a procedure(s) that controls the processes. Many companies include the servicing requirements under Section 4.9, Process Control, and avoid addressing this issue either in its quality manual or as separate procedures.

SERVICE PERSPECTIVES ON SERVICING

Interestingly enough, of the 20 sections of the standard, servicing is probably the least applicable to service organizations. That is because the classical definition of servicing refers to repairs provided by manufacturers to a customer after a warranty period has expired. Servicing also would apply if a retailer, such as a copier or computer retailer, provided extra services—usually considered an "extended warranty"—for an additional charge. Most service providers would find it more appropriate to use Section 4.9, Process Control, to cover their service operations. The wording in the 1994 edition of Section 4.9 refers to "production, installation, and servicing processes."

The easiest solution for service companies to deal with the requirements of Section 4.19 is to cover all of their servicing activities within Section 4.9, Process Control, and to write two sentences in their quality manual concerning Section 4.19. The two sentences should be:

- Our company does not provide servicing activities
- If, in the future our company does provide servicing activities, we will establish, maintain, and document a procedure(s) to satisfy customer needs and the requirements of the ISO 9001 standard

PRACTICAL EXAMPLES

- To maintain *"documented procedures for performing"* its service, a local computer store may give its technicians job aids to help them upgrade a customer's computer purchased from a national mail-order house.
- To provide *"servicing,"* a local copier retailer may provide a customer with a service contract to clean and stock toner on a monthly basis and to repair breakdowns within four hours.
- To verify and report *"that the servicing meets the specified require-*

ments," a roofer may agree to inspect replacement roofs once every two years.

COMPLYING WITH SECTION 4.19 IN SERVICE ORGANIZATIONS

Determine Need

Determine if there is a real need to identify servicing as a separate activity from Section 4.9, Process Control. If all activities can be reasonably covered within Section 4.9, write a disclaimer to that effect in the quality manual.

EDITOR'S NOTE

Section 4.19 typically is not used in service companies. An informal survey by the authors of registered service companies—and, interestingly enough, a survey of manufacturing companies—as well as registrars operating in the United States found little use of this section of the standard.

24

⁓⥃ ⥃⁓

Section 4.20,
Statistical Techniques

THE KEY QUESTION

Section 4.20, Statistical Techniques, asks:

1. Have we identified and are we using effective metrics, measurement techniques, and statistical tools to assess how well we are meeting the strategic objectives we identified in Section 4.1.1, Quality Policy?

INTERPRETING THE STANDARD

This section of the standard establishes two straightforward requirements. First, the company must decide what statistics it needs in order to control process activities and product characteristics. Second, the company must establish procedures to apply and control its application of statistical techniques. The standard specifically refers to *process capability*—measures of how well the system or processes are working—and *product characteristics*—measurements of the product produced. Differentiating between product and process reiterates ISO 9000's process focus, an orientation around how the work is accomplished. The basic theory underlying the standard is that by reducing variation and controlling processes, a good product or service will be produced. Too frequently, both manufacturing and service companies try to focus on product characteristics rather than on the processes that produced them. ISO sees both as important. This basic philosophy works equally well for service and manufacturing organizations. In fact, in keeping with the underlying ideas of ISO, process is more important than product, and both manufacturers and service companies should focus on metrics to help them judge how well they are carrying out their activities.

This section of the standard is critical to the success of any organization. It is the pivotal third step of the Shewhart Cycle—Check—when the differences between what we say we do (what our objectives are) and how we actually perform are identified. Measuring the effectiveness of processes and outcomes is fundamental to ensuring that customer needs are met and to running a company efficiently and effectively. Without measurement, management is left with guesses or "seat-of-the-pants" approaches. ISO auditors and registrars expect to see a direct tie between Section 4.20, Statistical Techniques, and the requirements in Section 4.1.1, Quality Policy, which requires the company to establish its objectives. Without this direct link between statistical techniques and quality objectives, it is impossible to judge whether the quality system is helping the company achieve its strategic goals. The quality objectives are, after all, wrapped into the strategic goals the company hopes to achieve in the near and long term. Statistics not only help assess how well the company is achieving its objectives, but help assess how well ISO registration is helping the company achieve its strategic goals.

It is important to note that the title of this section of the standard is Statistical Techniques, not statistical process control. Any measure, metric, or counting of any process or product measure meets the requirements of this section of the standard. Most service companies are likely to be gathering data in a wide variety of formats. These could be as simple as proportion of on-time deliveries, number of customer complaints, number of sick days used, variance from departmental budgets, or any other performance metric.

SERVICE PERSPECTIVES ON STATISTICAL TECHNIQUES

Service providers may have an advantage over their manufacturing brethren when applying this section of the standard to their processes. It is relatively easy for manufacturing organizations to focus on product characteristics, as required by the standard, and lose sight of the requirement to address process characteristics, also required by the standard. Because service companies frequently do not have a physical product on which to focus, they may be more naturally drawn to looking at their service processes, or at least not be distracted by a focus on product characteristics.

Service providers also have the additional advantage and broader vantage point of being accustomed to looking at qualitative as well as quantitative outcomes of their service processes. Customers' expectations are not limited to strictly quantitative or product metrics. Such things as customer perceptions of service personnel friendliness, helpfulness, promptness, and knowledge are qualitative metrics. One of the primary challenges facing service companies in an increasingly quality-conscious and quality-demanding market is figuring out which service characteristics customers value most and which are less important. It is not uncommon for a company to learn a hard lesson in the marketplace by focusing on outcomes that have relatively little value to their customers and thereby losing those customers to companies who have figured out what the customers really want.

Both service and manufacturing organizations must be careful of statistical phenomena informally known as *chicken efficiency* and *body counts*. Employees know their performance is assessed against certain metrics, and organizations can easily send an unintended message to their employees through these measurements that results in an outcome opposite from that desired.

"Chicken efficiency" is a label that came out of the experience of a fast-food franchise that tried to measure productivity by the amount of chicken cooked compared to the amount of chicken sold. The difference between what was cooked and what was sold— chicken efficiency—told the company how much product was thrown away. Store managers knew they were being assessed in terms of chicken efficiency. In an effort to make themselves look good, so as to control the flow of sales, they tended to leave the chicken in the ovens longer than required. As a result, the quality of the food decreased, customers became dissatisfied, and the company lost customers. The selected metric backfired in practice. Chicken efficiency has come to refer to a situation where individual employees recognize they will be measured against some standard and, in trying to meet the standard, take steps counter to the goal which the metric originally was designed to address.

The "body counts" label refers to asking employees to collect data that can neither be accurately gathered nor easily verified. The term comes from the war in Vietnam where the daily body count was seen as an important indication of how well the war was progressing. Commanders in the field were under great pressure to provide good news, and there was no easy way to verify the numbers of dead or injured. The body count results presented at the daily news briefing were routinely judged to be fudged. In both these cases, the metric selected provided no useful information or—at worse— drove down quality rather than helping the company achieve its objectives.

Service organizations can easily find themselves using metrics in counterproductive ways. For example, a company might decree that all telephone calls will be answered before the third ring. A hapless operator with more calls than he or she can handle may meet the quantitative objective by answering the phone within the required three rings, putting the caller on hold, and then trying to juggle responses for the various customers left on hold. The result is not the improved efficiency and happy customers the metric was supposed to ensure. In fact, the result is just the opposite—customers left sitting on hold and frustrated.

A similar situation arises when companies judge individual employees' performance against an average for all performances. A typical service example is to measure the time operators spend with each customer. The statistical average produced is used to judge individual operators' performances. Obviously, half of the operators will fall below the statistical mean, even if all of them are very productive and efficient. More important, in an effort to improve their numbers, operators may be inspired by this measurement to rush through calls and give inadequate service to customers. In total, the overall operational efficiency numbers may improve while driving away customers and reducing profits. The real issue is the company has not addressed the fundamental problem of the volume of calls and how to handle them efficiently and successfully. Good metrics should help the company identify problems and inefficiencies and to find solutions. If the metric doesn't provide that outcome, it is useless at best.

There are many problem-solving and process improvement techniques under the Total Quality Management rubric. Section 4.14,

Corrective and Preventive Action, is the ISO approach to process improvement and problem-solving. Regardless of the techniques used, metrics form the basis for fact-based decision making. A generic process improvement approach for service providers would be to identify:

- The critical aspects of the service important to the customer
- The steps or tasks necessary to satisfy the critical aspects
- The inspection and test points within the process that help ensure that the process is on track
- Opportunities for inefficiencies—opportunities for improvement—that are identified through the data gathered

Essentially, Section 4.20, Statistical Techniques, closes the loop from objectives to performance. The metrics collected and analyzed help the company improve processes and customer satisfaction, assess how well they are meeting their strategic objectives, and demonstrate the value of the ISO 9000 program to the company.

PRACTICAL EXAMPLES

- To *"identify the need for statistical techniques,"* an insurance sales organization may track customer "face time"—how long the salesperson is in front of a customer—as a way to help it assess the quality of its production objectives.
- For *"verifying process capability,"* a corporate trainer may interview trainees' supervisors six months after the individuals have attended a training program to determine if the attendees have applied the newly learned skills and if the training has helped employees improve their on-the-job performance.
- To *"control the application of the statistical techniques,"* a taxi cab service may track response time in its effort to meet an advertised quality goal to respond to telephoned requests for transportation within 15 minutes.

COMPLYING WITH SECTION 4.20 IN SERVICE ORGANIZATIONS

Identify Metrics Currently Collected

Companies typically collect data. Frequently, they do not know what data are being collected, how they are being reported, or how they are being used. Sometimes data are collected and not used. An ISO implementation project is a housecleaning opportunity. Just as in an examination of records for Section 4.16, and of documentation for Section 4.5, service companies need to identify which metrics they are collecting and eliminate those that are not useful or are counterproductive.

Select Metrics Important to Customers

Customers care about both quantitative and qualitative characteristics of services. Successful service providers determine customer needs and wants, provide the desired service, and use metrics to measure their success at providing the appropriate service. Techniques such as customer surveys, focus groups, and quality function deployment (QFD) are all techniques service providers use to determine customer needs and desires. Those needs and desires can be translated into metrics the organization should use to judge its performance and the performance of its ISO quality management system to help the company succeed.

Select Metrics Carefully

There is no requirement in ISO to create a massive statistical collection department, nor does it make intuitive sense to spend any more than the minimum necessary resources in gathering metrics. The real challenge is to select metrics that are efficient to gather and effective in providing the information needed. Also, it is important to ensure that selected metrics do not encourage employee behaviors detrimental to desired quality goals, such as chicken efficiency and body counts.

Use Statistical Techniques to Improve Processes

In addition to assessing how well the service company's ISO 9000 quality assurance process is working, statistical metrics should help the company improve its processes. Section 4.14, Corrective and Preventive Action, works best when a disciplined problem-solving approach based on facts and data is used to assess problems and opportunities for improvement. Management is used to dealing with data. By improving processes and judging the efficacy of the ISO program, Statistical Techniques is one way to help management understand the value and return of resources spent on ISO.

STATISTICAL TECHNIQUES IN THE CASE STUDIES

Measuring performance in service settings is either simple and obvious or exceedingly difficult. Some operations, such as counting items handled or processed, tracking on-time delivery, and other easily measured quantitative performances, lend themselves to statistical techniques. Other, less obvious qualitative metrics, such as customer satisfaction and loyalty, are not only difficult to collect and measure, they are difficult to define. Companies interviewed for case studies for this book revealed several general themes about how they approach the requirements for statistical techniques. They are as follows:

- Many companies gather various metrics as a matter of routine. Budget performance and team and individual performance objectives are typical of these metrics. A primary task in establishing an ISO program is to identify which metrics already are gathered and determine how they are reported and used. The next task is to determine which metrics are needed. The ISO standard requires the company to determine which metrics are required and to provide documented procedures to control their collection and use. The registered companies who shared information about their ISO experience did not report registration as a motivation to collect metrics. That is, in pursuing registration, these companies did not ask themselves, "What statistics should we gather so we can meet the ISO requirements?" These companies were already gathering useful metrics when they began their ISO registration process. Their task was to document and validate their collection and use.
- Service companies are vitally interested in qualitative measures, in addition to quantitative metrics. Such measures as customer service and market performance are at the heart of the performance of many service companies. Regular focus groups, test marketing, and customer follow-up surveys are all typical methods used by service companies to gather customer

service qualitative information. However, unlike more easily measured quantitative metrics, these qualitative measures may be harder to pin down, both in their definition of what is being measured and in terms of their measurement accuracy and results. Therefore, service companies should integrate their interpretation of these metrics with their intuitive sense of their customers, markets, and industry.

LESSONS LEARNED

Service companies report two primary lessons learned concerning Statistical Techniques. First, routine quantitative and performance metrics are relatively easy to gather but frequently are misused or go unused. Just as Section 4.5, Document and Data Control, and Section 4.16, Control of Quality Records, provide companies an opportunity to houseclean and eliminate unneeded documents and records, the ISO registration process gives companies an opportunity to review how they collect and use quantitative and qualitative metrics, to refine them so they can provide better information, and to eliminate those that are no longer useful.

Second, the companies reported that the ISO requirements dovetail with the growing marketplace emphasis on customer satisfaction and quality service. In many cases, they have been able to define a portion of customer service, for example, as time to response, minutes of wait on the telephone, numbers of billing corrections, and the like. Measuring these performance elements is not difficult, and the measurements over time are consistent and comparable. Other elements of customer service are qualitative. The companies interviewed reported that gathering valid, consistent, and qualitative information that actually measures customer service can be challenging. Because they are dealing in this with their customers' perceptions of their service, it takes thoughtful consideration of the measurement approach (surveys, interviews, focus groups), the questions that are asked, how they are asked, and how the information is compiled and analyzed.

It is important that you very carefully consider what you want to know and what you must ask to get answers to your questions. Industry benchmarks and best practices indicators are excellent reference tools to guide your own metrics choices. Further, they may serve as useful comparisons as you analyze or report your own findings. Universities and colleges have faculty or graduate students trained in surveying, interviewing, and other data-collection and data-analysis techniques, and they may welcome an opportunity to help you set up, evaluate, or analyze your metrics. Whatever your choice of procedures, your service company must focus on gathering such qualitative metrics in order to succeed in the marketplace. Registration to ISO 9000 and the requirements in Section 4.20, therefore, serve as a helpful inspiration to gather, evaluate, and use metrics.

Part III

This part of the book contains two final chapters. The first offers a series of proven practical strategies service practitioners can use to maintain and improve upon their ISO program. The second chapter contains information about planned changes anticipated in the Year 2000 revisions, along with resources for quality practitioners to keep abreast of these changes. It also contains several appendixes, including one listing resources available to help service companies as they develop their ISO registration program.

25

~ ✦ ~

Life After Registration

Hooray and Congratulations! You've accomplished your goal. Now think ahead to the time when, after much effort and commitment of resources, your service company has achieved ISO registration. If you are not planning to become registered, imagine a time of confidence in which your company is in compliance with all of the requirements of the ISO standard and could become registered if a decision was made to seek formal registration. Now the key question becomes, "Is there life after ISO registration?" or "How can we continue to maintain the quality and productivity gains we have achieved?"

ISO registration is like a garden. It requires ongoing routine attention and care in order to bloom into a healthy, self-sustaining entity. This chapter contains a dozen strategies that will help you and your colleagues maintain the enthusiasm and focus necessary to keep your ISO program on track and blooming vibrantly.

ONE

Ask your registrar to conduct semiannual rather than annual surveillance audits. Most registrars contract on three-year cycles, beginning when you have achieved registration. As a general rule, the registrar will visit once or twice each year to conduct a surveillance audit, depending on how your company negotiates your contract. Many companies elect to have an annual surveillance audit based on the notion it is less expensive to host an audit once per year. Although there are indeed some savings associated with travel expenses for the auditors, such an approach proves to be penny-wise and pound-foolish.

Your registrar must conduct a complete audit of the entire system within the three years of your contract. The registrar can conduct three audits and cover one-third of your processes during each audit, or can conduct six audits and cover one-sixth of your processes during each audit. The shorter, more frequent audits are generally easier and less disruptive to the company's operations. More importantly, frequent audits help everyone in the company stay focused on maintaining the ISO systems. Additionally, if by chance your ISO program suffers a breakdown and the registrar does not visit you for a year, you will have a more difficult time repairing your system and bringing it back into compliance. In all of these scenarios, annual rather than semiannual audits may turn out to be more expensive than originally estimated.

Two

Ask your registrar before the surveillance audit what kinds of difficulties he or she routinely sees when returning to a company. The response will give you a good idea of the kinds of things he or she is looking for and also the kinds of difficulties companies face when maintaining their quality assurance processes. Your registrar also can provide you with industrywide data concerning nonconformances found both in initial registration audits and ongoing surveillance audits. Registrar auditors are becoming better able to predict areas in which companies typically have difficulty complying with the requirements of the standard, as ISO gains acceptance in the U.S. marketplace and as data and information about its application become more readily available.

In the early years of ISO, for example, many companies struggled to maintain up-to-date documentation. As more consultants and trainers have gained experience with documentation, fewer companies find difficulty in this area. Armed with information about the most common areas of concern, you can make a point of first focusing your attention on areas most likely to be a concern to your registrar. Also, you should make a special point to conduct more frequent internal audits in these areas of probable concern.

THREE

Your continuing requirement to operate an ongoing internal audit program under the requirements of Section 4.17, Internal Quality Audits, is one of the most powerful ideas in the standard. Internal audits work to your advantage to keep your ISO process in tune. You should be scheduling internal audits for each month or six weeks during the year. This schedule should be established so at the end of the year, you have looked at every requirement of the standard against every affected function or activity at least one time. You should also examine your management reviews and statistical techniques for ideas of areas of concern you might include in your internal audits. Your primary goal in conducting internal audits should not be to find negative things or to perpetuate the current systems. Your primary goal should be to predict potential areas of concern and to find opportunities for improvement. Some companies make the mistake of reducing the frequency of their internal audits after they become registered. This is counterintuitive and detrimental to both your ISO program and the general well-being of your quality management program. Frequent audits will keep the program visible and help keep everyone focused on the need to maintain and nurture their ISO systems. Reducing internal audits to quarterly or even semi-annually schedules puts too much burden on your internal auditors to do a thorough job. Reducing the audit schedule also sends a message to employees that they can slack off between audits.

FOUR

It is a good idea to update your annual audit schedule every quarter, or at least semi-annually, to take into account any changes in systems, people, or processes. There is a requirement to schedule audits based on "the status and importance of the activity to be audited." New equipment, new processes, employee turnover, unexpected problems, degradation in service in specific areas, missed deadlines, or any negative results are all indications of potential areas for improvement that should fall within the internal auditing cycle. It is also a good idea to schedule audits in areas that are succeeding. Your validation of these successes gives your internal audit team an opportunity to recognize and support processes and people who are doing good work.

FIVE

Consider changing the name of your internal audit team to *an internal assessment* team and tying their efforts together with a process improvement effort. Several process improvement techniques and programs are available to help companies seek and develop efficiencies in processes. These apply a variety of quality tools and approaches, ranging from quality circles to team awards offered by individual companies, professional organizations, and individual state-managed awards. More than 40 states have established programs or foundations to encourage quality programs in businesses. Some programs also include team award initiatives. For example, the Excellence in Missouri Foundation manages both a Malcolm Baldrige-like state business award program and a process improvement team award similar to that promoted by the Association for Quality and Participation. The ISO 9000 standard and your internal audit program, serve as an excellent self-assessment tool, as well as a foundation from which to seek opportunities for improvement. Changing the name from internal audits and folding the program into a process improvement program also helps eliminate the fear commonly associated with audits, and puts a positive perspective on the effort. There is no requirement in the ISO standard to specifically call your internal audit program by that name. Nor is there a requirement that the program be a stand-alone or separate activity. Your organization must accomplish the goals and satisfy the requirements of the standard. What you name the program or how you accomplish the goals is strictly up to you.

SIX

Conduct ongoing training for your internal audit team. The ISO 10011 Guideline on how to operate an audit program suggests you provide additional or continuing training for auditors. This training can be organized and structured any way that seems reasonable and helpful to your auditors. It could be short meetings every two or three months, or it could be a four-hour meeting every six months, in which you bring your auditors together to discuss lessons learned and to share success stories. It is also a good idea to ask the auditors to help one another by conducting role-plays and sharing strategies they have learned while conducting audits. To encourage interaction, provide snacks and sodas during the training and create opportunities for the auditors to share their experiences, rather than trying to lecture to them or review information they already know.

SEVEN

Work to change the focus and emphasis of your corrective and preventive action program from corrective action to preventive action. Corrective action is reactive and seeks to correct existing problems. Preventive action seeks to predict potential problems and eliminate them and, further, seeks to identity and enhance efficiencies in work processes.

Obviously, your company must seek and correct identified errors and inefficiencies. Unfortunately, however, sometimes this effort is negatively construed by individuals whose area is under scrutiny. Corrective action sends a subtle message that individuals have failed or are not performing tasks adequately. In truth it is frequently the system—or lack of an efficient system—that has failed. Regardless, changing the focus from corrective to preventive action will help reduce this negative connotation. Individuals are usually willing and enthusiastic about finding easier and more efficient ways to accomplish their tasks. An assertive preventive action program will capitalize on this willingness and enthusiasm.

EIGHT

Use your management review and statistical technique efforts to improve your processes. Management understands how to use data and judges the success of any effort on positive numbers generated. Also, although there are intangible benefits from an ISO system that will encourage and satisfy employees as they gain experience with your program, senior managers often best understand quantitative data, such as metrics and trends.

There is no requirement for determining the cost of quality in the

ISO standard. However, a discussion in the ISO guidelines of how to assess return on investment for quality programs can help you think about and address this issue. Another reason to collect and process quantitative data is that most process improvement and team award programs insist on data collection and evaluation of outcomes as a measure of success. The statistical techniques you select and use should be directly tied to the goals and objectives you determined for the company and the goals established for functions and individuals within the company. Figuring out which data to collect to get appropriate, useful, accurate, and meaningful information to support your program is a challenge. Without the data, however, once you receive your registration certificate, there may be little management motivation to continue to support and use your ISO program.

NINE

Use your ISO program as the foundation for other related quality initiatives. More than 40 states have quality initiatives, many based on the Malcolm Baldrige National Quality Award. Because there is significant overlap between the requirements of ISO and the Baldrige, an effective ISO program will serve you well as an initial step toward a Baldrige-based state program. Many industries also offer award and recognition programs, and a growing number of customers conduct such programs for their vendor companies. Successful quality practitioners are able to see the similarities among the various quality tools and techniques, and are able to parlay the strengths and achievements established in one program to address a new program.

TEN

Remember that your ISO system succeeds or fails on the basis of the people involved. Do not become so enamored with and wrapped up in processes you forget about the human side of how work is accomplished. Look for opportunities for small celebrations. Most individuals appreciate frequent small recognitions rather than elaborate and infrequent ones. Make these sincere and grounded, since most individuals recognize phony recognition that is not based on real achievement. Reward and recognition programs are one way to express appreciation and support your ISO program and to motivate everyone to maintain a high level of enthusiasm for its goals.

ELEVEN

Communicate, communicate, communicate. Use every available opportunity to keep the ideas and purpose of your quality management program in view. Signs and posters, notes on bulletin boards, company news articles, brief e-mail messages addressed to everyone, quality briefings tied into or as a short part of routine meetings and training programs are some of the avenues to keep the ISO idea visible and to keep individuals focused and motivated. It is true that the squeaky wheel gets the attention. You must find ways to communicate what is happening with the program, particularly the successes of the program, to keep it vibrant.

TWELVE

Keep smiling. If anyone tries to tell you any of this is easy, turn and run away because he or she obviously doesn't know what he or she is talking about. If it were easy, everyone would be doing it.

LESSONS LEARNED

During the writing of this book, we have learned much about ISO and how service companies apply the requirements of the standard. We have learned a great deal about how to translate the manufacturing and product-related concepts and terminology of ISO into useful ideas for service providers. However, this remains a significant challenge. Our case study interviews have been a rich resource of information and insight into the practical aspects and on the daily tribulations and small victories quality practitioners in service companies have experienced and achieved.

The most dominant recurring theme and lesson learned throughout is that for these companies and others, their quality system—whether it's TQM, process reengineering, ISO 9000, quality circles, quality tools, team awards, or the Malcolm Baldrige National Quality Award—share a focus on application of a solid problem-solving process. It is a process of critical thinking, using a simple set of tools to guide identification of problems or opportunities, evaluation of current condition and risk, assessment of alternatives, decision making, and implementation. Although sometimes the process is frustrating, leading us into blind alleys, and sometimes people misapply the techniques or fiddle with the data, this systematic approach helps us identify goals, deal with challenges, and sustain our knowledge gains. The ISO standard is especially powerful in helping service companies organize and manage thoughtfully. Where there are failures to successfully apply ISO, these are related to individuals who fail to or are unwilling to use the tools correctly, not because there is a problem with the methodology. Dedicated people who sincerely try to build and sustain a quality management system are the winners, not only in achieving their objective goals, but also in the personal and group growth that they achieve in the process.

On that positive note, congratulations on your decision to adopt the ISO standards and good luck on your ISO journey.

26

~⟩ ⟨~

The Year 2000 ISO 9000 Family of Standards

The International Organization for Standardization has been investing tremendous efforts to make the planned Year 2000 revision of the ISO 9000 family of standards more useful to quality practitioners. The ISO 9000 quality standards are the basis for about 200,000 large and small quality systems in 120 countries, in manufacturing and services, and in public and private sectors around the world. It is vitally important for the continued growth, acceptance, and success of the ISO 9000 standards that they meet the evolving needs of quality practitioners. These efforts include making the document more user-friendly and easier to understand and apply. Such improvements are particularly good news for service organization practitioners who have struggled with the manufacturing focus and terminology of prior editions.

As a matter of routine, ISO reviews and revises each standard and guideline once every five years. This is a very large undertaking because more than 11,000 ISO standards and guidelines cover most manufactured products. As most of these standards and guidelines focus on the technical aspects of particular types of products, the review and revision process is based primarily on such engineering usability and manufacturing issues as compatibility of designs.

The ISO 9000 family of guidelines and standards—currently about 24 different documents—focuses on quality processes, however, not products. Therefore, review and revision of these standards and guidelines has required a different approach. This chapter contains information on the current development of the revised

ISO 9000 standards. The chapter also lists several resources available to help quality service professionals keep abreast of the proposed changes.

The original version of the ISO 9000 family of standards was published in 1987 and revised in 1994. The next revision is scheduled for release in late 2000 or early 2001. There were some important changes between the 1987 and 1994 versions. In addition to some wording changes, the 1994 version required companies to draft a quality manual that describes their quality system, and added the requirements for quality planning (Section 4.2.2) and for preventive action (Section 4.14). These changes helped practitioners overcome the misconception that it was necessary simply to document methods used, without concern for customers' needs and continuous process improvement. The basic structure of the document did not change between 1987 and 1994, however.

The planned changes for the Year 2000 revision reflect the continued effort to strengthen the focus on customers' needs and continuous process improvement. Associated with this is an effort to make the organization and structure of the documents more compatible with each other. Several components are related to this effort.

First is the planned elimination of the ISO 9002 and 9003 standards; a single 9001 quality assurance standard will take their place. Second, management guidance will be included in a new ISO 9004 guideline. The goal is to develop consistency between the one standard and the one guideline. The single standard will establish the quality assurance requirements, and the single guideline will address the broader topic of quality management. This guideline will include information to help practitioners address those requirements in the standard that do not apply to their particular organization.

Third, the numbering system used within the various guidelines and standards will be coordinated. The ISO 9004 Management Guideline will be revised so its numbering system coordinates with the sections in the ISO 9001 standard. This will allow practitioners who are looking for information on document and data control, for example, to use the same section number to find the relevant information in both the standard and guideline. In previous editions, it was necessary to use a cross-reference matrix to locate information related to each topic in various standards and guidelines.

And, fourth, there is an effort underway to coordinate the ISO 14000, the environmental family of standards, with the ISO 9000 family. Currently, there are many similarities and areas of overlap between the requirements in both the quality and environmental standards, particularly for auditing, documentation, records, and management oversight. This movement to coordinate the two families will allow practitioners to avoid redundancies in addressing requirements and, more importantly, will allow registrars to conduct joint audits of both standards during one visit. Because this is such a daunting task, it remains to be seen whether ISO is able to coordinate the two ISO families—9000 and 14000. However, committees have been formed and work is underway to achieve that goal.

The International Organization for Standardization has undertaken two extraordinary steps in the Year 2000 ISO 9000 revision process as they work to make the documents more user friendly. First, in 1998 ISO conducted a worldwide survey—they received 1,120 responses from 40 countries—asking practitioners about their experiences with the standard and what changes they would like to see to make the standards more useful. The seven most requested changes were:

- Simplify language and terminology
- Facilitate integration into one management system
- Address continuous improvement
- Use a process model approach to quality management
- Improve compatibility with other management system standards
- Address customer satisfaction more strongly
- Make the standards more business oriented

The survey results also provided the technical writing committee with feedback on which sections of the standard were most important to practitioners and which sections were most difficult for practitioners to apply to their business operations. According to the survey, the five most important sections of the existing standard are:

- Section 4.14, Corrective and Preventive Action
- Section 4.1, Management Responsibility
- Section 4.9, Process Control

- Section 4.17, Internal Quality Audits
- Section 4.13, Control of Nonconforming Product

The five most difficult sections to interpret and apply were:

- Section 4.4, Design Control
- Section 4.20, Statistical Techniques
- Section 4.14, Corrective and Preventive Action
- Section 4.9, Process Control
- Section 4.2, Quality System

The results of this worldwide survey concerning the most important and the most difficult to interpret sections mirror the experiences described in the case studies presented in this book. Service providers should note that the key elements (often the most challenging elements) of ISO are consistent with the key elements of other quality management programs, such as the Malcolm Baldrige National Quality Award, TQM, team empowerment, and Six Sigma quality approaches. This idea emphasizes the powerful way in which many service practitioners can use the ISO standard as a foundation for any quality management system and/or can incorporate current quality practices into their ISO program.

A second interesting approach adopted by ISO as part of this change process is the notion of pre-release "test drives." This new two-part program includes a survey of companies around the world that will solicit their assessment of the new Year 2000 standard, and will give selected companies an opportunity to implement the new standard and report on its usefulness in improving business results.

These remarkable efforts by the International Organization for Standardization to make the Year 2000 ISO 9000 family of standards more user-friendly are good news for service organizations. They reflect a realization on the part of ISO and other standards organizations around the world—such as the American National Standards Institute, the U.S. member of ISO—of the high stakes involved and importance of the ISO 9000 series to quality practitioners. The ISO 9000 series has been moving away from a narrow engineering and product manufacturing focus to a broader quality management program useful to non-manufacturing service organizations. This has spread its base and acceptability to many different organizations, including small- to medium-size manufacturing and service companies, and non-profit and government organizations. The surveys and pre-release testing indicate an understanding by the standard writers to address the concerns of the variety of sectors now using the standard.

The key question for service organizations of course is whether they wait until 2000 to begin to work on an ISO 9000 registration project. The answer—most emphatically—is no! There are several reasons why service companies should start their ISO programs now:

- Business is not going to stop and wait until the year 2000. Companies need to have good quality systems in place to support their business now, and the current ISO standard will help them continue to achieve their strategic business goals.
- The Year 2000 ISO 9000 family of standards is currently scheduled to be released in late 2000 or early 2001. Given the complexity of this worldwide effort, this date may slip to mid-year 2001 or later.
- Most of the essential requirements in the Year 2000 ISO 9000 family of standards will be the same as currently existing requirements. It is still too early to anticipate which and how many of the requirements will change. While the number and location of requirements is likely to be adjusted in the new standard, the fundamental issues to be addressed will remain essentially the same.
- Companies that are registered to the 1994 standard will have six months to a year to upgrade their existing quality processes to meet the requirements of the Year 2000 ISO 9000 revision after the new standard is issued.
- There is no time like the present!

Several excellent quality journals and World Wide Web sites report on quality and ISO, some of which are listed in the appendix at the end of this book. Two resources particularly useful for quality practitioners interested in keeping up with changes in the Year 2000 ISO 9000 family of standards are:

- http://www.iso.ch—The International Organization for Standardization's Web site posts news releases on the status of the Year 2000 ISO 9000 update project.
- http://standardsgroup.asq.org—This is the site for the Amer-

ican Society for Quality standards group, which is charged by ANSI with administering the standards committees; they also post news releases on the progress of the revisions.

Because the revision to the ISO standards will not be finished until the next millennium, quality practitioners should periodically check these sources for updates on the revision process.

Appendix A

ン茶 だ

The Key Questions

Here is a summary of the Key Questions contained in each chapter. These questions are designed to help service company practitioners begin to think about issues to address as they begin their journey to ISO registration. The Key Questions will also help the service company's internal audit team begin to form a way to assess the current and continuing status of their quality management program.

Service companies seeking registration must address each requirement in the ISO 9001 or ISO 9002 standard. The requirements are clearly identified by the word "shall." There are 138 such "shalls" in the ISO 9001 and 119 "shalls" in the ISO 9002 standard. Companies must address each "shall" in a way that satisfies their own internal service processes and satisfies the needs of their customers. Two things provide challenges for service companies. One is that the language of the ISO standard is arcane at best, and second, the concepts have a manufacturing orientation. Service practitioners must translate this language and focus into terms familiar to themselves. The Key Questions are examples of how this translation may be accomplished, and give readers an idea of the kinds of questions they can develop for themselves.

One of the easiest ways to begin an ISO transformation project is to highlight each of the "shalls" in the standard and then to translate the statement into a question. For example, Section 4.6, Purchasing, says you "shall evaluate and select subcontractors on the basis of their ability . . ." That statement can be changed to a question: "Do we qualify our subcontractors and vendors based on their ability. . . ?" By using this technique, the ISO team will immediately generate 138 questions for the ISO 9001 or 119 questions for the ISO 9002 to start their assessment. The project does not stop there, however. Once the initial requirements are identified, the team must begin to examine the company's processes in greater depth and detail.

As the team gains experience, they will continue to generate more in-depth questions, and may—over the years—generate several hundred questions that will help the team self-assess how well the company's quality management process is supporting their needs to satisfy their customers. The Key Questions in this appendix provide a start on that process.

Section 4.1, Management Responsibility

- Has management established its strategic vision and does everyone in the company understand the vision?
- Is management successfully using its quality management system to achieve its strategic objectives?

Section 4.2, Quality System

- Is management effectively using a quality system that meets the requirements of its customers, its employees, and the ISO 9000 standard?
- Does the quality system provide a way to "Say what you do, Do what you say, Check the differences, and Act to correct the differences?"

Section 4.3, Contract Review

- Do we understand what our customer wants?
- Have we agreed with the customer what is needed?
- Can we deliver—do we have the capability to deliver—the service our customer wants?

Section 4.4, Design Control

- Do we have a good way to plan how we design the tasks and steps we must do to perform and to control our service processes?

- Do we incorporate customer requirements and satisfy legal or statutory codes as part of the design process?
- Is everyone who is affected—or potentially affected—by our service included in the design of the service?
- Do we periodically review the design processes and do we run pilot tests to make sure our service will satisfy our customers?

Section 4.5, Document and Data Control

- Do we have procedures, work instructions, and other documents that help us do our work?
- Are we sure our procedures accurately describe how we do our work?
- Are procedures and work instructions available and useful to everyone who needs them and does everyone use them?
- Do we know that everyone has the up-to-date procedures and work instructions they need?
- Is the documentation we use reviewed and authorized for use by knowledgeable and responsible persons?

Section 4.6, Purchasing

- Do our vendors understand our needs?
- Are our vendors able to provide the products and services that we need?

Section 4.7, Control of Customer-Supplied Product

- Are we protecting things—such as products, services, or information—that our customer gives to us and we use in the service we provide back to our customer?

Section 4.8, Product Identification and Traceability

- If we need to, can we identify our service or the components of our service?

Section 4.9, Process Control

- Do we know what we are doing and how work gets accomplished?
- Are we consistently providing excellent service to our cus-

tomers through our ability to control our own internal work processes?

Section 4.10, Inspection and Testing

- Do we know what we are supposed to do to receive products and services into our company, and are we doing it?
- Do all our employees check their own work as they do it and before they pass it on to the next person along the service chain?
- Before we finalize the service, do we know it is right?

Section 4.11, Control of Inspection, Measuring, and Test Equipment

- Do we know what we need to measure, and do we have the measurement equipment we need to provide our service?
- Do we know that our measurement equipment is capable of measuring what we want it to measure?
- Do we know that our measurement equipment is accurately measuring what we think it is measuring; that is, is it properly calibrated?

Section 4.12, Inspection and Test Status

- Have we carefully thought through the steps necessary to provide the service and identified planned stop points to ensure that the work is being completed satisfactorily?
- Do we know if one step in our service process has been completed and/or inspected as correct before we begin the next step in the process?

Section 4.13, Control of Nonconforming Product

- If something is wrong, do we take necessary steps to make sure the error does not continue through the work process and, further, make sure that it does not go to the customer?
- Do we: identify; document; evaluate; segregate; dispose of; and notify persons affected; when we have a failure?

Section 4.14, Corrective and Preventive Action

- When something is identified as wrong, does the individual responsible make sure the problem is resolved?
- Do we effectively and efficiently handle customer complaints and comments?

Section 4.15, Handling, Storage, Packaging, Preservation, and Delivery

- Can we carefully handle, package, store, preserve, and deliver physical components of our service so they reach our customer undamaged?
- Can we protect our people while they handle, package, store, preserve, and deliver physical components of our service?

Section 4.16, Control of Quality Records

- Do we know which records will demonstrate the successful completion of our service?
- Are our records legible and useful?
- Do we provide safe storage, and can we retrieve records when we need them?

Section 4.17, Internal Quality Audits

- Are we effectively using an ongoing self-assessment process that helps us maintain and improve our work processes?
- Are we able to demonstrate that we "Say What We Do and Do What We Say?"
- Is there a process in place to conduct systems and compliance assessments to demonstrate that an effective ISO 9000 program is helping our company reach its strategic goals?

Section 4.18, Training

- Do we know what training and experience our people need to do their jobs successfully?
- Do we provide the training or ensure our people have the experience they need?

Section 4.19, Servicing

- If we supply service under a servicing contract, do we know what processes we need and whether those processes are effective and efficient?

Section 4.20, Statistical Techniques

- Have we identified and are we using effective metrics, measurement techniques, and statistical tools to assess how well we are meeting the strategic objectives we identified in Section 4.1.1, Quality Policy?

Appendix B

❧ ❦

Terms

One of the primary difficulties service organizations face as they apply ISO is its manufacturing terminology. The following short list of terms and definitions translates some of this terminology into jargon-free and user-friendly definitions service practitioners can use. Another source of definitions is ISO Guideline 4802, which provides official definitions of important terms. Most standards and guidelines also offer some definitions.

Customer

The individual or company that purchases a product or service from a supplier is the customer. Service companies generally have an inherently clearer understanding of their customers than do manufacturing organizations, which sometimes focus on products and practices. Although ISO does not specifically address internal customers, it is essentially impossible to become registered without having a coherent internal company system that recognizes the need for all departments and functions within the organization to cooperate and to satisfy their internal customers, in addition to their external customers.

Internal, External, and Extrinsic Audits

The activities represented by these terms sometimes are referred to as first-party, second-party, and third-party audits. Internal audits—first party—are done when an organization examines itself, its own procedures and processes. Customers or potential customers frequently conduct second-party—external—audits of vendors to evaluate their suitability. Extrinsic, or third-party audits, are conducted by companies—such as registrars—that provide this service as an independent and unbiased verification of the company's quality assurance system.

Objective Evidence

Objective evidence refers to verifiable statements of fact, records, or observations of performance or activities that demonstrate the quality system is being used. Objective evidence provides the foundation for fact-based solutions to problems and continuous improvement activities.

Quality Control and Quality Assurance

Quality Control (QC) is an inspection process. It seeks to identify errors and correct them. QC is reactive to problems. Quality Assurance (QA) is a management commitment to structure work flows and processes to control variability and reduce waste and errors. QA is proactive and aims to prevent problems. ISO is a QA system.

Registered and Certified

These terms are frequently used interchangeably. However, companies that satisfy the ISO requirements technically are registered to ISO and listed in a master directory currently maintained by Irwin Professional Publications. The confusion in terminology occurs because registered companies receive a certificate of registration from their registrar.

Registrar

A registrar is a company accredited by one of several world bodies to conduct third-party audits and to issue certificates of registration to ISO. The Registrar Accreditation Board (RAB) in the United States, United Kingdom Accreditation Service (UKAS) in the United Kingdom, and Raad voor Accreditatie in the Netherlands are three large accreditation agencies. There are also accreditation agencies in France, Germany, Australia/New Zealand, Ireland, and Japan.

Specified Requirements

The ISO standard specifies requirements in the form of the 138 shalls companies must address and satisfy. Companies further are subject to government, regulatory, and professional organization requirements. Customers may include specific requirements in contracts or in other expressions of their expectations. Regardless of who specifies them, an ISO-registered company must satisfy the requirements placed on it.

Subcontractor

The supplier purchases components, materials, supplies, or services from a subcontractor or vendor.

Supplier

The standard refers to the ISO-registered company as the supplier. The supplier is the company that satisfies the ISO standard requirements and becomes registered.

Appendix C

✿

Resources

THE WORLD WIDE WEB

The World Wide Web is filled with resources related to ISO 9000. Any search engine can find numerous sites devoted to the topic. There are also some interesting mail list-servers available. Be careful, however, when searching, to include "9000" along with "ISO" to avoid entrance into the far fringes of cyberspace inhabited by lonely souls "In Search Of . . . ."

American National Standards Institute (ANSI)

http://www.ansi.org
ANSI is the United States member of ISO, and this is its homepage.

American Society for Quality (ASQ)

http://www.asq.org
This formerly was the American Society for Quality Control. It recently changed its name to more accurately reflect the ideas of quality management in contrast to quality control. ASQ holds the Secretariat for ANSI, which means it is the administrative arm for all things related to ISO and the standards. ASQ also holds the Secretariat for the National Institute of Standards and Technology (NIST), which administers the Malcolm Baldrige National Quality Award. You can order copies of the standard from them. Also, for

less than $100 a year, a membership in ASQ will bring you the excellent *Quality Progress Journal,* which tracks all news related to the quality movement. Membership will also cause your mailbox to overflow with information from vendors about their quality-related products and services. You can write to ASQ at 611 East Wisconsin Ave., P.O. Box 3005, Milwaukee, Wisconsin 53201-3005, or phone 800-248-1946.

Association for Quality and Participation (AQP)

This national organization sponsors many quality initiatives, including its annual regional and national Team Excellence Award program. Its *AQP Journal* is well written and thoughtful. Most importantly, it takes a *people* rather than a process-and-systems approach to quality issues. Service organizations will find the terminology and approach used by AQP inviting and supportive. You can contact AQP at 801-B West 8th Street, Cincinnati, Ohio 45203-1607, or phone 513-381-1959.

The International Organization for Standardization (ISO)

http://www.iso.ch/

This is the official homepage. It contains information about each member country and the current status of committees and standards. It will also answer questions.

The ISO Handbook

Robert W. Peach has updated this useful handbook over the past several years. It contains a series of short articles and information on many ISO topics and is a wealth of ready reference and information on every imaginable topic related to the ISO standards. The articles are easy to read, interesting and informative. You can pick it up and begin reading anywhere and learn something new. It is available from CEEM Information Services, Fairfax, Virginia 22032, or phone 800-745-5565.

The ISO Standards

The following standards are available from ASQ:

ISO 9001. Order it rather than ISO 9002, even if you might decide to pursue registration to ISO 9002. They are the exact same document (except 9002 does not require Section 4.4, Design Control). It is a good idea to know what Section 4.4 says even if you do not comply with that part of the standard. Your registrar auditors will be thinking about those issues and you need to be prepared to understand the difference. Other useful ISO publications include the following:

- ISO 10013, a guideline on developing quality manuals. It offers a basic summary.
- ISO 10011-1, 2, 3, Guidelines for Auditing Quality Systems. Part 1 is an excellent foundation for any audit program. It describes the duties and responsibilities for all the participants in an audit, along with the parts of an audit. Part 2 describes basic auditor training and experience needs. Part 3 presents information on how to organize and manage a quality audit program. The guideline is an excellent foundation to organize any audit program and is a good start on developing a procedure for your internal audit program.
- ISO 9004-1, Guideline for Management of a Quality Assurance System, helps companies understand how to manage an ISO program.
- ISO 9004-2, Guidelines for Services, helps companies apply ISO to service organizations.
- ISO 9004-4, Guideline for Quality Improvement, helps to create and use an effective corrective and preventive action program.

List of ISO Registered Companies

McGraw-Hill Quality Systems Update, Burr Ridge, Illinois (800-353-4809), provides a quarterly update of all companies in North America registered to ISO. The listing is organized by Standard Industrial Classification (SIC) Code, and alphabetically. It lists company names and relevant contact information along with the scope of the company's registration. The list also identifies all registrars operating in North America.

The Service Auditor's Ultimate Checklist

This checklist of questions helps service auditors think about how to gather objective evidence to assess a service organization's quality management processes. The checklist contains 600-plus questions drawn from the ISO 9001 Quality Standard, the 1998 QS-9000 Automotive Standard, the ISO 9004-2 Guidelines for Services, and the ISO 10011-1, 2, 3 Guidelines for Auditing. All questions are specifically tailored to translate the requirements into terms and issues relevant to service functions. Available from The Trainers Workshop, 1-800-598-9009.

Quality Resources

The folks who publish the book that you are reading produce many other fine titles on ISO, quality topics, and related topics. Their homepage address is http://www.qualityresources.com.

Russ and Tracy Russo

We are always delighted to hear from our readers. If something we said confused you, if you want to ask a question or offer an idea or suggestion, you can contact us via e-mail at: russ@charropubs.com. If you prefer snail mail, we can be reached through Charro Publishers, Inc., P.O. Box 3442, Lawrence, Kansas 66046-0442.

Appendix D

꧁ ꧂

Contact Information

Chapter	Title	Contact Information
5	4.1, Management Responsibility	General summary
6	4.2, Quality System	Sheridan van Asch, Senior Executive Officer TAFE Queensland Brisbane, Queensland, Australia
7	4.3, Contract Review	Joe McMillan, Director of Quality Dittler Brothers, Inc. P.O. Box 848 3915 Old Mundy Mill Road Oakwood, GA 30566 Phone: 770-539-5436 Fax: 770-539-5005 email: mcmiljo@dittler.com
8	4.4, Design Control	Richard Jones, President Richard Jones Management Consultants, Inc. 413 Briarwood Drive Kingston, Ontario K7M 7V2, Canada

		Phone: 613-389-3475 Fax: 613-389-7559 email: rjmci@shadow. kingston.net
9	4.5, Document and Data Control	Gregory Lawton, President Lawton-Russell, Inc. 311 South Wacker Dr. Suite 1750 Chicago. IL 60606 Phone: 312-236-0500 Fax: 312-551-6446
10	4.6, Purchasing	Jack Davis, Nurse Clinician Drs. Mark Figgie and Richard Laskin 535 E. 70th St. New York, NY 10021-4892 Phone: 212-606-1041 Fax: 212-249-4653 email: davisj@hss.edu
11	4.7, Control of Customer-Supplied Product	Arch McFarlane BC TEL Education Burnaby, British Columbia, Canada

12	4.8, Product
	Identification and
	Traceability
		Raymond Berta, President
		Applied Consumer and
		   Clinical Evaluations
		2575B Dunwin Dr.
		Mississauga, Ontario
		   L5L 3N9, Canada
		Phone: 905-828-0493
		Fax: 905-828-0499
		email: rberta@acceintl.com
		homepage: www.acceintl.com

13	4.9, Process Control	Thomas J. Spitznagle, Vice
		   President of Strategic
		   Planning

Health Risk Management, Inc.
8000 W. 78th St.
Minneapolis, MN 55439-2536
Phone: 612-946-7520
Fax: 612-946-7694

14 4.10, Inspection
and Testing

Sally D'Angelo, Manager
 Client Services Support
International Language
 Engineering Corp.
Boulder, CO

15 4.11, Control of
Inspection,
Measuring, and
Test Equipment

Don Hurd, Owner
Snelling Personnel Services
4200 W. Cypress St.,
 Suite 480
Tampa, FL 33607
Phone: 813-877-4300
Fax: 813-877-5854
email: rrsr20a@prodigy.com

16 4.12, Inspection and
Test Status

June Peckingham, Quality
 Management
 Representative
Charles River Saab
570 Arsenal St.
Watertown, MA 02172-2897
Phone: 617-923-9230
Fax: 617-923-9834
email: crsaab@crsaab.com
homepage: www.crsaab.com

17 4.13, Control of
Nonconforming
Product

Beverley S. Schalon,
 Laboratory QA/ISO
 Coordinator
Lake Charles Plant
PPG Industries, Inc.
Lake Charles, LA
e-mail: schalon@ppg.com

18	4.14, Corrective and Preventive Action	Becky Harper, Programs and Planning Manager Americas Customer Support Center Austin, TX
19	4.15, Handling, Storage, Packaging, Preservation, and Delivery	Chad Thompson, Corporate Packaging Engineer United Parcel Service 1 UPS Way Hodgkins, IL 60525 Phone: 708-387-4562 Fax: 708-387-4555 email: prx1ck+@is.ups.com homepage: www.ups.com
20	4.16, Control of Quality Records	General Summary
21	4.17, Internal Quality Audits	Don Freer, Customer Service Quality Manager Dow Chemical Company Customer Service Organization 2030 Dow Center Midland, MI 48674 Phone: 517-832-1127 Fax: 517-832-1150 email: dfreer@dow.com
22	4.18, Training	Mary Kay Hopkins, CRB Mary Kay Hopkins, Inc. REALTORS 120 S. Ryan St. Lake Charles, LA 70601-5951 Phone: 318-439-1079 Fax: 318-436-0678 email: mkh@mkh.com homepage: www.mkh.com

| 23 | 4.19, Servicing | No case study |
| 24 | 4.20, Statistical Techniques | General summary |

Index